REMEMBRANCE

REMEMBRANCE

RUSSIAN POST-MODERN NOSTALGIA

ALEXANDRE GERTSMAN
GENERAL EDITOR AND CURATOR

GRISHA BRUSKIN • ERIC BULATOV • GENIA
CHEF • VLADIMIR CLAVIJO-TELEPNEV
• VITALY DLUGY • SEMYON FAIBISOVICH •
RIMMA GERLOVINA & VALERIY GERLOVIN
• ILYA KABAKOV • NAUM KAZHDAN •
KOMAR & MELAMID • SVETLANA
KOPYSTIANSKY • ALEXANDER KOSOLAPOV •
BORIS MIKHAILOV • NATALYA NESTEROVA •
MICHAEL ODNORALOV • LEV POLIAKOV
• OSCAR RABIN • MIKHAIL ROGINSKY •
LEONID SOKOV • SLAVA TSUKERMAN • OLEG
VASSILIEV • VLADIMIR YANKILEVSKY

"...THERE IS NOSTALGIA FOR CULTURE AND FOR THE DESTRUCTION OF CULTURE; A LONGING FOR REFINEMENT AND FOR VANDALISM..."

ALEXANDRE GERTSMAN

"...PAINTINGS WERE THROWN INTO DUMP-TRUCKS OR RUN OVER BY BULLDOZERS..."

EDWARD LUCIE-SMITH

"...THE PROBLEM OF ACHIEVING AN AUTONOMOUS IDENTITY AND STRONG SENSE OF SELFHOOD HAUNTS RUSSIAN ART..."

DONALD KUSPIT

"...THERE WERE SUCH ISLANDS OF DEATH IN A NUMBEROF EX-SOCIALIST COUNTRIES..."

SONYA ABADIYEVA

"...THE FORMATION OF A COLLECTIVE IDENTITY LEADS TO A VISION SKEWED TOWARD NATIONAL VALUES..."

KATHRIN BECKER

"...FIGURES THROB, TRYING TO BRING ORDER OR HARMONY INTO THEIR UNSTRUCTURED ELEMENTS..."

ALEXANDER BOROVSKY

"...THE PEOPLE BLINKED AND SAW THEIR EMPIRE, IMPOSSIBLY EQUAL PARTS OF MYTH AND REALITY, WAS GONE..."

JEFFREY LIPSCHUTZ

This book has been published in conjunction with the traveling exhibition
Remembrance: Russian Post-Modern Nostalgia. The exhibition debuts in Summer 2003
at the Yeshiva University Museum – Center for Jewish History, and travels throughout
the U.S. and Europe through 2005.

General Editor and Curator: Alexandre Gertsman
Production Editor: Clark Gard
Production Assistant: Xenia Pachikov
Designer: Niamh O'Hara
Art Director: Nikola Zabev
Imaging Director: Tyrone Toral

IntArt - International Foundation of Russian and Eastern European Art, Inc.
782 West End Avenue - Suite 122
New York, NY 10025
Telephone 212.663.2363; Facsimile 212.663.2396
Website: www.intart.org; E-mail: info@intart.org

ISBN: 1-889948-00-4 soft cover
ISBN 1-889948-01-2 hard cover
Library of Congress Cataloguing and Publication Data

With 116 illustrations, 88 in color.
Unless otherwise indicated, all catalogue illustrations and exhibition works have been
provided by IntArt.

Front and back covers: "Suffering" series (detail), Vladimir Clavijo-Telepnev (1999-2002)
Inside front cover: *The Broken Tree* (detail), Oleg Vassiliev (c. 1992)
          Alex and Marianna Dogot Collection
Inside back cover: *Foro Imperiale* (detail), Genia Chef (2001)

Prepress and printing by DataPons – Skopje, Macedonia
Printing organized by the Prima Centar for Applicable Knowledge and
          Creative Development
Printed and bound in Macedonia

CONTENTS

Preface and Acknowledgments

What is the function of memory as it relates to the creation of the abstract construct we call "culture," and how does art participate in the development of cultural memory? The IntArt Foundation's "Remembrance" exhibit brings together many of Russia's most prominent contemporary artists to explore exactly these sorts of questions.

Inspired by the rigorous deconstructivist methodology of post-modern theory, this exhibit seeks to call into question the supposedly finite distinction between past, present, and future, and assert a fluidity of cultural thought that links undeniably our historic past with our cultural future. The uniqueness of the "Remembrance" exhibit, which unlike most exhibits does not unite around a particular artist or stylistic school, is that it brings together a myriad of personal histories and artistic modes with the same conceptual goal in mind – to examine the ways in which Russian culture has been and is still being influenced and (re)created by a kind of artistic collective memory.

Russian artists exist today in a state of physical and cultural transition. Dealing with issues such as the fall of the communist Soviet Union, emigration out of their Russian homeland, and the rebuilding of a federation of capitalist democratic states, Russian artists find themselves and their country to be multidimensionally transitional. This transition comes in many forms, but universal to this transitional state is a murkiness of past, present, and future that challenges both the artist and the viewer to examine what it means to be in the *present* – a place that owes its existence to the past and its survival to the future.

The art contained in this exhibition is expressive of this unique cultural transition. It is impossible to separate these artists and their works from the cultural heritage that is their individual and national history. For this reason, contemporary Russian art of any medium or subject is intrinsically and undeniably nostalgic, meaning that there is an element to any sort of artistic comment on the present direction of Russian culture that is necessarily backward-looking.

The works of art found in the "Remembrance" exhibit are vehicles for their creators to explore the meaning of culture and question the existence of art and culture within a socio-historical context. Each work of art encourages the onlooker to interact individually with his or her own cultural past, and in doing so, to remember.

A project of this scope could not have been realized without the cooperation of number of individuals and institutions, beginning with the trustees of IntArt - International Foundation of Russian and Eastern European Art, whose financial and moral support have made the tremendously stressful job of directing an art foundation considerably more manageable. Personal thanks are owed especially to Marianne Wyman, Chair of the Board of Trustees, and Professor Robert Cancro, Member of the Board, for their her help in organizing the multi-month "Remembrance" festival of Russian art and culture surrounding the New York exhibit premiere.

The success of this exhibition and catalogue is also due in part to the generosity of museums and private collectors who allowed the IntArt

Foundation to borrow for display and/or reproduction works for the "Remembrance" project. I would like to thank the following people and the institutions they represent for their contributions to this project: Dr. Alla Rosenfeld - Department of Russian Art, Jane Voorhees Zimmerli Art Museum, New Brunswick; Dianna Cross - Metropolitan Museum of Art, New York; Mikki Carpenter - Museum of Modern Art (MoMA), New York; Kimberly Bush - Solomon R. Guggenheim Museum, New York; and Alexis B. Smith - Pace/MacGill Gallery, New York. I would also like to thank Yuri and Nelly Traisman, Robert and Gloria Cancro, and also Mr. and Mrs. Mark Wilf for allowing works from their private collections to join the exhibit, in addition to Nadia Dlugy for lending her late husband's works.

In addition to the members of the IntArt Board, there are several arts professionals associated with other institutions to whom credit is due. First, I would like to thank Sylvia A. Herskovitz and Reba Wulkan at New York's Yeshiva University Museum, who encouraged the development of this project from the beginning, and who are hosting the "Remembrance" premiere. Next, I would like to thank Sonya Abadiyeva the Museum of Contemporary Art, Skopje, for welcoming the IntArt Foundation to Macedonia and helping to establish a promising new dialogue with the Balkan artistic community.

For developing unique and thought-provoking writings that elevate this book beyond the level of a mere *catalogue illustré,* I would like to thank the authors of the essays that appear in this book: Edward Lucie-Smith, Donald Kuspit, Sonya Abadiyeva, Kathrin Becker, Alexander Borovsky, and Jeffrey Lipschutz. In addition to thanking the authors of the inspired writing that appears in this book, I must also thank the brilliant translators who made these essays accessible to the exhibit's Anglophone audience: Antonina W. Bouis, Lynn Visson, Janina Dubizhanskaya, and Alexandra Ilievska.

For providing invaluable support to the Foundation and its various projects, I would like to give an extremely heartfelt thank you to Xenia Pachikov and Eduardo Solis. Without your help the Foundation would not be where it is today.

I am hugely indebted to the people who worked tirelessly on the direct production of this catalogue. It took a trans-continental team of hardworking creative minds to put this book together, and it is with pride that I can say that this is the best IntArt publication to date. In New York: Niamh O'Hara and Tyrone Toral; in Skopje: Jovan Balov, Kornelija Koneska, Vasco Evkoski, Nikola Zabev, and everyone else at the Prima Centar and DataPons – your hospitality and professionalism made our trip to Macedonia an undeniable success.

Finally, I would like to thank Clark Gard for overseeing the production of this catalogue. I can say with utmost sincerity that this project would never have come together without your countless hours of work; from cover to cover, your presence is on every page.

Alexandre Gertsman
Curator of the "Remembrance: Russian Post-Modern Nostalgia"
President and Founder of IntArt – International Foundation of
        Russian and Eatsern European Art, Inc.

NOSTALGIA AND MYTH IN RUSSIAN ART • ALEXANDRE GERTSMAN

There is a uniquely Russian attitude anchored in a visionary understanding of the past. In it, the future guides the understanding of the past, and the cultural heritage of the Russian avant-garde from the 1910s through the 1930s is but one of the isles of imagination from which this "nostalgic conceptualization" draws its many lives. Artistic comprehension of the future is manifested in the form of an idealistic dream, characteristic of Russian culture. The dreamlike quality of this artistic approach to time (history, the future, etc.) means that each artist is working within a conceptual framework that is necessarily mythic. Drawing from folkloric old-Russian stories and symbols, emotions and sympathies from tsarist Russia (which is in itself historicized to the point that fact blends with legend), as well as the current reality of the Communist experiment and its aftermath. Artists on the contemporary Russian scene are both coping with and employing to their creative benefit a unique mixture of the concrete and the abstract, the atheistic and the religious, the socio-historical and the fictive-mythical. The dream, originally utopian in essence, produced both an idyllic spirituality, and a rather "pastoral" capitalism. This dream of the future which began with Dostoyevsky and Chekhov and runs down through the literary modernism of Andrey Belyi and, later Evgeny Zamyatin, takes on the form of typically Russian gnoseological idealism, a pre-Orwellian prophecy to which the Bolsheviks gave an extreme manifestation.

Russian post-modernism did not reject utopia. Rather, it transformed it into an original and eclectic matrix. Modern Russian artists continue to be enthused by some utopian constructions that they find extremely attractive. The idea itself is always ambivalent, since post-modernism is by nature deconstructivist, while the idea of "a great utopia" tends towards the Hegelian, the flipside of deconstruction, and the idea of the so-called "Absolute." This ambivalence, characteristic of Russian art, reflects the duality of our time. Yet, both western modernist art and western "academic" Conceptualism bluntly reject such ambivalence, such temporal dualism. Rather, they view the sources of the conflict in political administrations-in government-but not in human nature and not in the mental structure of social relations. Ultimately, Russian art is more inclined than is Western art toward a prophetic intonation. At the beginning of a century, the great dream of the next century is in effervescence. One of humankind's grandest utopian dreams marked the twentieth century – a dream of a great commune and of a great nation. Virtually the entire century was lived under the banner of that dream, and was ironically characterized by an endless struggle against that dream. Now, with the communist dream finally having succumbed to the struggle, there has emerged a clear and paradoxical nostalgia for its disappointed ideals.

In order to understand the contemporary period more fully, one should look at the last fin-de-siecle. In the Russian art of the nineteenth century, artists of the *Mir Iskusstva* (World of Art) movement – Constantin Somov, Borisov-Musatov and, to a certain extent, Alexander Benois – based their art on reminiscences of the eighteenth century. They were nostalgic: remembering a world that no longer was. However, this remembrance turned out to be also prescience of the art of the *future*. Mannerism in its time also constituted a decadent Renaissance, and painting at the end of the nineteenth century amounted to the decadence of the Victorian Age. It appears that such trends in art at the end of centuries are universal. In art, decadent sentiments seem to create the basis for a new artistic vision.

Russia, one of the cradles of avant-garde art, contributed to the world the key principles of modernism by exporting explosive and shocking ideas.   Although France and Germany were indeed home to early modernist experiments, these found their first serious theoretical expression in the beginning of the century in Russia, where they evolved into mature modernism.   Wassiliy Kandinsky developed German expressionism into a non-figurative abstraction. He was the principal theorist of modernism and influenced the likes of Piet Mondrian and, while teaching at the Bauhaus, Paul Klee and Hans Hoffman. Aleksei Yavlensky, by his abstractions, influenced French art at the beginning of the century, as did Natalia Goncharova and Mikhail Larionov early in 1911 with their Rayonism (non-subjective abstraction). The constructivists Vladimir Tatlin and El Lissitsky anticipated the Bauhaus School of Design and Art, the ancestor of contemporary design and architecture. In 1912, Marc Chagall with his absurdist subjects anticipated by several years the Surrealism of the 1920s. Naum Gabo and Anton Pevzner contributed to the first theories of modern sculpture, as did Archil Gorky who anticipated abstract expressionism at the beginning of the 1940s in America and contributed to the downfall of modernism. These Russian artists and others were responsible for the creation of the aesthetic of the twentieth century.

At the onset of the twentieth century, Russian culture was characterized by the coexistence of the art of the social dream with the art of the decadents. In poetry, there was Vladimir Mayakovsky, and there was Anna Akhmatova. In literature, there was Maxim Gorky, and there was Andrey Belyi. In painting, Kazimir Malevich, and Konstantin Somov coexisted. The theater saw both Vsevolod Meyerkhold and Konstantin Stanislavsky, while music produced both a Dmitry Shostakovich and an Alexander Scriabine. Given such dualism, the Russian avant-garde reflected an exacerbated vision of a new world, of a new objective in art. Despite its ideological dogmatism and the limited nature of its vision, this period of Russian art laid the foundations for contemporary Russian post-modernism. It is in fact the idea of using old traditional forms to create new, vibrant artistic elements, the idea of post-modern eclecticism and the deconstructionist system of thought, that are at the core of a unique trend in today's Russian art.

Russian artists today are similar to their predecessors in that they take the initiative in transforming the mental mechanisms of art-making. Of course, the art world of the former Soviet Union was isolated from world culture and Russian artists relegated to the absorption of new trends and movements from the dynamic American and European art schools. With emigration, however, the nascent underground movement began to make major contributions to world culture. While Russian artists today want to preserve elements of national Russian culture, they are also participants in an eclectic cosmopolitanism that is avowedly Russian.

During the 1960s and 70s, the Soviet government oppressed unofficial art and there was no possibility of it being exhibited. While in the 1960s western artists such as Robert Smithson and Michael Heizer were using bulldozers as tools to create works of art, in the Soviet Union the government was making use of them for the physical destruction of works by underground artists shown at unofficial outdoor exhibitions.

Ironically for many underground artists, the 1960s and 70s were the most creative times of their artistic lives. The situation of official isolation estab-

Rimma Gerlovina & Valeriy Gerlovin
a2 + b2 = c2, 1990
(color coupler print, 19" X 19")

Rimma Gerlovina & Valeriy Gerlovin
BE-LIE-VE, 1990
(color coupler print, 19" X 19")

lished a unique spiritual environment for creativity, and provided primary material for the imagination. Artists cultivated inner strength in their quest of self-expression and thus created their own Aesopian language. Immigrant life in the satiated land of capitalist countries opened new grounds of creativity for some of them, while the breakdown of the Soviet Union and the communist regime completed the process for both emigres and those still left in the former Soviet Union. Artists who did not base their art on political themes made the transition to freedom and democracy with far more ease; the others were in a more difficult situation.

Contemporary Russian painting is not only conceptual but also academic. It is a conception of the dream of painting. This is visible in the work of artists like Vitaly Komar and Alexander Melamid, Semyon Faibisovich, Natalya Nesterova, Michel Odnoralov and Oleg Vassiliev. This eclectic blend makes Russian post-modernism unique and special, a separate path running parallel to the highroad of development of western post-modernism. This path can prove extremely fruitful for it offers interesting modalities for the development of art in the future.

Although Russian painters live in a resolutely post-communist world, their work, in its exceptionally varied forms, reveals the privileged position of the early twentieth-century Russian avant-garde, just as the creative roots of artists in the Renaissance summoned pagan antiquity. It is characteristic of Russian post-modernism that entire "chunks," quotations of typical visual images, or individual objects build a new system of objects. For example, from the ordinary surroundings of a Soviet communal apartment Ilya Kabakov creates a new environment, unique and incredible in its detail and innovation. The photographer Boris Mikhailov transposes ordinary pieces from daily life or landscapes into a phantasmagoric spiritual experience. Russian post-modernism, with its unconscious duality and ambivalence, should be of special interest to the contemporary art world primarily, but not solely, because of its parallel development vis-a-vis Western post-modernism. Russian artists exist within a traditional structure of emotions with a desire for Utopia and yet, they destroy it. Those artists with more philosophical-ethical views tend to oppose the politicized approach of Western Conceptualists, who are inspired by a more pragmatically coded perception of the world.

If it is possible to see that a certain "ghetto mentality" is peculiar to artists as it is to creative people in general, it is especially true of contemporary artists born in the ex-Soviet Union now living all over the world in the "Diaspora." Invariably, in communist Russia, they tried to create a self-imposed mental, psychological ghetto, an "internal emigration," in order to isolate themselves from the totalitarian regime under which they lived. Now, having broken away in the 1970s and 1980s from the old regime to live in the United States, France, Germany, or in a deeply-changed Russia, the participants of this exhibition have developed an ambivalent feeling of nostalgia for the condition of psychological pressure created by the official Soviet apparatus. Russian artists like to toy with historical traditions, building upon them and tearing them asunder at once. Their ideas, ambivalent towards and contradictory of past art, are simultaneously nourished by it. More often, Western artists employ the traditions of the past as playful elements suitable for destruction. Russian artists play this "game" with a strong spiritual attachment to the past. At the same time, both Russian and

European post-modernists carry in their selves an element of "romanticism-in-destruction" perhaps linked to Proustian "lost time."

Conceptualism in Russian art has some special nuances due to the form of its rejection of the past. Western Conceptualism finds emotional inspiration in a categorical aesthetic rejection of its cultural inheritance and carries within itself a thirst for its own constant distraction. Russian Conceptualism deconstructs its cultural inheritance, but with unconscious elements of nostalgia and respect for its ideological heritage as one can especially see, for example, in the works of Kabakov, Komar and Melamid, Kopystiansky, Roginsky, and Sokov. Deep in their souls, Russian artists love and revere the old culture. This purity derives not insignificantly from Russian spiritual tradition. Russian artists are literary in their creativity and preserve an instinctive, ineradicable reverence for art created by their centuries-old culture. Even when they effectively destroy that art which they love, they cannot destroy their nostalgia for the past.

Russian Conceptualists actively use the traditions of early modernism and create a "Nostalgic Conceptualism," which combines deconstructive tendencies with a yearning for order and "lost truth." Russian Conceptualism is metaphysically, rather than politically, emotional. The ideas of Russian artists, in the majority of cases, are not slogans, but signs of spiritual motion. If American Conceptualism is often politicized and based on populist ideas, Russian Conceptualism emphasizes the metaphysical traditions of Russian spiritual life. The moment of rejection of traditional academic art is very specific in its creativity due to the subconscious respect it has for it. This is especially interesting because traditions of the Russian Jewish Ghetto and "communist Ghetto" are interlaced with the historical tradition of the old Ghetto and of serfdom.

In order to achieve creative freedom, the artist has to fully live - then overcome - the feeling of being confined. This pseudo-masochistic path to liberation is characteristic of ex-Soviet Conceptualists. Russian Conceptualism is unique because, while fiercely denying past culture - a denial of the so-called "democratic" but all too suppressive regime - they carry the traditional Russian secret respect for a strong state: a habit of dealing with the absence of the freedom to choose, and thus of using allegorical language. What makes their creativity most characteristic and interesting is its symbolism. Unlike with American conceptual art, in which the symbolism is consumptive (a la Baudrillard), Russian symbolism uses the aforementioned Aesopian language to treat *political* symbols.

Some of these artists reflect not only the "two-world" position of those who struggled to create art under conditions that limited what, by the definition of the state, would be regarded and accepted as art, but also a "three-world" condition. They ask what relationship, if any, exists between the fact of being "strangers" in their own society and the other aspects of their existence. The issue became, ironically enough, more rather than less complicated by Perestroika and the breakdown of the Soviet state.

The works of Rimma Gerlovina and Valeriy Gerlovin are dominated by the symbolism of the past, of the mythical and the archaic, of the primordial sign. They deconstruct a semiotic symbol through its visual decorative ornamentation. They question the future through the deconstruction of "hiero-

Komar & Melamid
The Wings Will Grow, c. 1996
(silkscreen on paper, 30" X 30")

Komar & Melamid
Judith on the Red Square, from "Nostalgic Socialist Realism" series, 1993
(oil on canvas, 36" X 36")
Robert and Gloria Cancro Collection

glyphs" and symbols of the past, transforming them from ancient "countenances" into a visual design of the future. The sign as the initial element of a word and the word as the initial element of a sign are their favored, ambivalent paradox. The hieroglyph and sign, characteristic of the Gerlovins, give rise to an interesting interpretation of a "Renaissance-style" approach combined with an "Old Testament" element. There is a play of sign and sense, sense and feeling, visual image and emotional element. They create visual images of hidden thoughts by the words of their "anthropomorphic" poetry.

Ilya Kabakov is an artist who creates myth, primarily myth of the past. His myth, however, does not correspond to historical reality. The artist depicts a world of mythical pseudo-history, with absurdist tales dating back to the literary tradition of Daniil Kharms and the Oberiuts. The past, present, and future are transformed into a nihilistic, absurd interpretation of truth and time. He brings us an absurdist pseudo-historic tale about the past endowed with seemingly precise historical details. He creates a myth, providing non-existing quotations, sayings and books. Kabakov contrasts the future with a history that is unreal, and utterly fantastic. The more realistic the historical details, the less genuine the actual historical concept. His exploration of the accompaniment to his installations, constructions, and models became one of the main subjects of Kabakov's works. Later, he invented an interesting model of "Character," in which the artist proclaimed his ideas through the eyes of a "created" person. It was as if a person, in the Soviet Union living in the solitude of his own privacy and psychologically isolated from official life, was trying to express his true thoughts through pseudo-official representation(s). He developed his conceptual ideas into so-called "Moscow communal existence," creating a pictorial, linguistic, and behavioral language of life in communal apartments in the Soviet Union, an absurd world with metaphysical reminiscences.

Eric Bulatov's works mark a conceptual image in space. Not in the space of Soviet communal flat-life, but in the space of a romanticized Soviet landscape, of propaganda drawings and geometric forms hailing the Russian revolutionary poster and the Constructivism of the 1920s. Those images, slogans, and phrases create a facsimile of Soviet history and of the psychology of Soviet life. But the space in Bulatov's works is much more abstract than the art of the Russian avant-garde, and is turned into an almost hieroglyphic structure. This combination of geometry and pseudo-romantic landscape creates an emotional atmosphere of anxiety, fear, and instability of Soviet existence in its social milieu.

Bulatov's work sometimes has a poster-like blatancy, while other times it is abstract with elements of visuality that move from geometric forms, to cognitive forms manipulating the viewer. He creates an atmosphere of taciturn portent tension through an intense scrutiny of a few objects. While his paintings are signals from a mythic space, they remain very concrete, expressive and prepared by the artist for immediate perception by a viewer, like the light of a stoplight. In his more communicative landscapes, each element—house, cloud, ray of light—creates a directed movement, a rhythm that seems to turn the artist's conceptual ideas into concreteness. The concrete details of his landscapes escape earthly depiction, flying up to the sky, scattering in space, as if to signify events without giving their realistic character; the realistic elements of his works play, in this case an auxiliary role.

This is not a conceptual story retold, not a playful paradox, but a signal whose roots lay in Futurist thought, entwined by external methods of revolutionary propaganda, static depictions of nature, and historical architectural reminiscences. All these elements are subsumed under the main goal of showing the hierographic structure of the signal and the creation of an emotionally charged atmosphere through a semiotic perception of the world.

Vitaly Komar and Alexander Melamid produce works that investigate myth on both historical and stylistic levels. They simultaneously imitate both style and an absence of style. Their Sots-Art has its roots in the traditions of Russian genre painting and the Russian *Peredvizhniki* as well as in the objects of Dada. Komar and Melamid address various historical events, treating them with both sarcasm and a feeling of nostalgic decadence, constructing multi-layered compositions. The viewer finds in their paintings from the *Nostalgic Socialist Realism* series a combination of conflicting objects that illustrate the essence of their deconstructive methods. In *Nostalgic Socialist Realism*, the artists find a balance in the eclectic admixture of originality and banality. They combine ideas of modernism with traditions of American street graffiti, ironically juxtaposing the high and the low, the ancient deified form with Pollock-like sarcastic strokes of artistic irony. What is dominant here are parody splashes of light, the pseudo-opulent atmosphere of a theater, as well as an exaggerated drawing and political-extremist symbols. In this series, Komar and Melamid demonstrate a deconstructive endeavor in destruction of the harmonic aesthetic system.

In their paintings, Komar and Melamid combine an academic treatment of the figures with elements of technical primitivism. Komar and Melamid conduct a search for compatibility of different artistic systems and, at the same time, for a possibility of their nihilistic destruction. There is an interesting adjacency here: nostalgia for culture and for the destruction of culture; a longing for refinement and for vandalism. Komar and Melamid have turned to various events in the history of Europe in the last century, treating some aspects with irony, some with sarcasm, and some with a sense of nostalgic decadence. It is easy to find in the works of Komar and Melamid combinations of contradictory objects, illustrating the essence of their deconstructivist methodology, which often amounts to the recognition of famous historical personages, or the triumph of pagan reason. Like Kant's ambivalence between philosophical categories and logic and Bakhtin's analysis of Rablais with his carnivalesque atmosphere wavering from the high to the low, Komar and Melamid demonstrate fluctuation from exploitator to exploited, and from the highly spiritual and moral to the atheistic and base.

The photographs of Boris Mikhailov, devoted to both the past and the present, attempt to represent a huge and sweeping mythical picture. He scenographically combines various mythic indicators to form monstrous images of a distorted and *sub*real past. Rather than attempting solely to expose and unmask, he also creates his own eschatological world. His works show a unique, ambivalent, and subtle play of spirit and flesh, fallen and exalted. All the details for his sets come from real life; they are familiar or recognizable, and yet now they combine in such a way so as to metaphysically disorient the viewer. The specificity of his photographs translates to a deconstruction of the notion of historical existence.

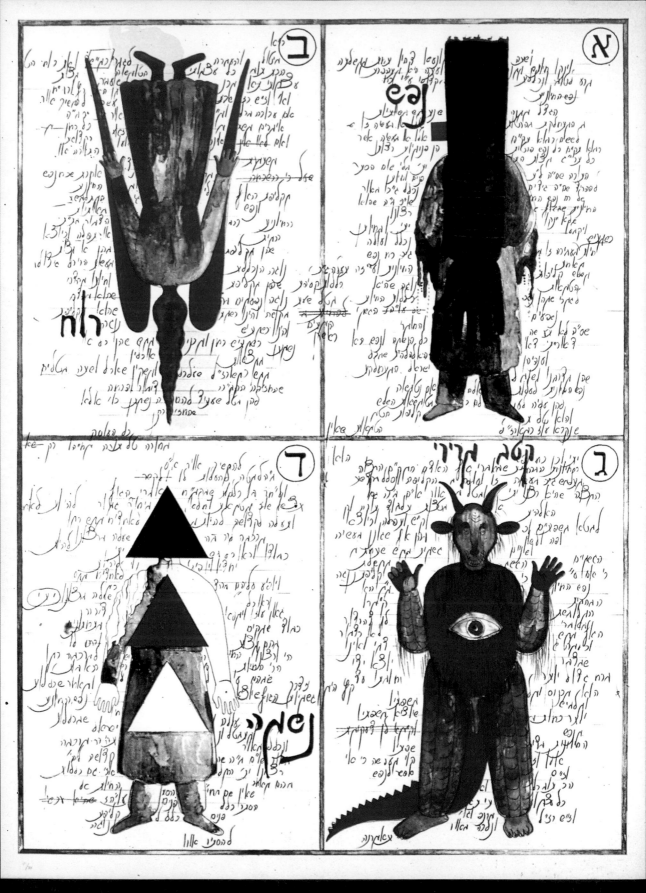

Grisha Bruskin
Woman With a Model of the Lenin Mausoleum and *Marshal with a Missile*,
from "Life is Everywhere" series, 1998-99 (porcelain, height 8")

His series of kitsch or "lubok-like" photos with painted ornamentation, for example, deconstruct the pseudo-romanticism of false Soviet idealized life, transforming it into a pseudo-historical and utopian dream. The color symbolism of these photos illustrates the absurdity of this artificial world with a blunt Dadaist sensibility. Dadaist devices, which deconstruct kitsch photography, blend with Sots-Art folklore, creating a chimerical world of fantastic objects within a closed space. His series *Dances* recreates both a real and shadow world. The dancing living figures are ghosts from the past, from a world of nonexistent being. They are real and concrete, but simultaneously similar to symbolic signs of that world which has disappeared. The nostalgic lyricism of the series is linked to the theme of destruction and death masked by forced gaiety, an imitation of vital energy and emotion. By creating his mythical world on an almost trop-real/quotidian foundation, Mikhailov's works investigate the drama of being, that uncertainty of the future which characterizes our era.

Lev Poliakov portrays ordinary life, and, through the cosmopolitan powers of observation like those of Henri Cartier-Bresson, creates a nostalgic portrait gallery of individuals ranging from the Nobel Prize winner Joseph Brodsky to the poet Anna Akhmatova to peasants at a market and a worker on the street. Yet all of these figures remain self-contained, distinct individuals, regardless of Communist attempts to annihilate individuality. Polyakov's portraits of the leaders of the Communist party at Soviet parades and the KGB prison courtyard appear gray and faceless, memorials of a time gone by but forever engraved in the memory of the living. Polyakov creates a nostalgic gallery of Russian life in flux, images of past and present, permeated by the unique spirit of the land in which the photographer was born. His photographs are therefore very personal, and are in a sense unofficially autobiographical accounts of his homeland. Polyakov, like Milton Rogovin, is interested not in the creation of aesthetically pleasing picture photographs but in the protagonists of his works. He consciously does not seek external formal effects in the composition, and concentrates instead on the documentary aspects of the object-plot. Polyakov the documentarian stands alone among the groups and tendencies of contemporary photography. In his works, the beautiful dialogue between art and nature of nature is liberated from a particularized historical context.

Leonid Sokov
Lenin-Artist, c. 1985
(oil on canvas)

Alexander Kosolapov, who for three decades has been living on the border of two cultures, one American and one Russian, works on the concept of the "integration" of communist and capitalist consumer cultures or, to be more precise, on forms of post-communist consumption. Co-opting Warhol's concept that "the epitome of [American] beauty is McDonald's," Kosolapov searches for a Russian product that epitomizes beauty similarly. In Kosolapov's opinion, it is easier to explain Russian culture to an American viewer through recurrent motifs of national culture. Accustomed to manipulating social iconographic signs from contemporary society such as Mickey Mouse, Lenin, the Marlboro trademark, or such Russian icons as the hammer and sickle, or red star, Alexander Kosolapov transports the Kalashnikov into the ranks of the symbolic phenomena of our age.

A constructivist element stemming from the Russian avant-garde and uniquely interwoven with folk-art underlies the Sots-Art of Leonid Sokov. The tradition of the Russian "lubok" (a cheap, mass-produced print) and other articles of peasant culture, are framed in artistic compositions whose formal structure goes back to the tradition set by Tatlin. Employing Sots-Art ironic reminiscences, Sokov offers a unique blend of formalist aesthetics and ancient popular "life in action." His works are not merely parody, for they display the down-to-earth and sharp humor of the "lubok." They are iconographic both in terms of artistic stylistics and in the political and social semiotic of the individuals portrayed, who often unite two cultures - Russian and American. One work has Stalin with Marilyn Monroe; another shows Lenin and a Giacometti character.

Alexander Kosolapov
Mickey-Lenin, 2002
(bronze, height 50")

Grisha Bruskin, like many of his contemporaries, examines folkloric sources, and also has an interest in the Kabbala as well as a clear interest in Sots-Art and Soviet symbolism. This represents the linking of two nostalgias. The central theme of Bruskin's work is *books*, linked in particular to his interest in Jewish culture and other "religions of the Book." Thinking about his work as book-centric explains why he never produces just a single painting but always a series. One series of his works is even characterized by lines resembling the pages of a book, in some of his canvases, and Bruskin even uses excerpts from Hassidic texts in a few of these paintings. For example, in *Metamorphoses*, Bruskin includes a text in ancient Kabbalistic characters from the 18th century titled, "Lets Talk." When the excerpts from the book line up on his canvases, the obscure writings become *text*. The same part of a whole construction is seen in Bruskin's figurative images of Kabbalistic entities with their often-dismembered bodies, enlarged and mystical, as if subject to pictorial exorcism. The Kabbalistic series is not simply a series of logically connected paintings, but rather a collection of entities that act as a lexicon, a dictionary, or an encyclopedia.

It is rare indeed to find in contemporary Russian art to find a vision as original Kopystiansky's combined with her vividly-expressed affinity for Russia. Kopystiansky possesses both an emphatically national originality and a philosophical Conceptualism based on the classic Russian "provincial nostalgia" for distant metropolitan culture. The artist creates the abstracted image of a "romantic young lady" that discerns, in books and magazines, echoes of the large world's breathing. Svetlana Kopystiansky skillfully plays upon her invented "provincial naivete" which radically distinguishes her from a multitude of mutually resembling artists and makes her art fresh and devoid of banality. Kopystiansky's idea is to combinine the utility of day-to-day reality with a nostalgic and romantic dream. Her concept originates in the art of Russian avant-garde artists of the early twentieth century such as Vladimir Tatlin and Velemir Khlebnikov.

Svetlana Kopystiansky uses symbols that are unembellished and free of artifice and therein remains faithful to the "provincial dream" that has more recently defined her art. Kopystiansky's ideas have a day-to-day specificity, also characteristic of the art of Mark Chagall, which is, in general, a common trait amongst artists who work with various aspects of provincial life. Compare, for instance, Kopystiansky's works with Chagall's *Soaring*, paying particular attention to the romanticizing of provincial towns found in the latter's work. Kopystiansky has very a similar intonation so Chagall in her romantic treatment of rustic themes. Where the two artists diverge is in the psychological approaches they take to romanticized provinciality; unlike Chagall, who used his art as a further vehicle for exploring his own (Vitebsk-based) provinciality, Kopystiansky is linked to her provincial routes *exclusively* through her art, and is otherwise urban-escapist.

Leonid Sokov
Marilyn and Bear, 1989-90
(mixed media on paper, 22 1/2" X 30 1/2")

Alexander Kosolapov
Lenin and Stalin with Marlboro, 1996
(lithograph, 18" X 24")

Mikhail Roginsky began absorbing international art ideas while still in the Soviet Union in the 1960s. Unlike Komar and Melamid, or Kosolapov, immigration to France in the late 1970s did not change his perception of the art world. After the move, Roginsky switched his focus towards his new environment, and developed his ideas on the contemporary art spiral. Roginsky expressed interest in the regular and often banal objects of everyday life as early as the beginning of the 1960s and has often been described as a Russian Pop-artist. Original American Pop Art consisted of removing an object from its original context, transplanting it, and re-instating it as a piece of trash produced by society. Roginsky connected with Pop-artists in their belief that objects are symbols of monotony. However, in his works the subject is not a consumer product, but solely an everyday object that is at the same time functions metaphysically. Very often, by abstracting the subject from the viewer, he restores the central meaning inherent in the object (unlike the case of American Pop Art, which served ultimately to reveal the intrinsic meaninglessness of the "art objects" it employed).

Oleg Vassiliev
From "Home With an Attic" series, 1991 (lithograph, 29 3/4" X 21 1/2", each)

Roginsky's illustrations center around the 1960s and 70s, a time of ugliness, disorder, and communal apartments (all subjects of the artist's investigation). Roginsky found an artistic beauty in their ugliness without depicting them in beautiful "commercial" techniques (again in contrast with the American Pop Art paradigm). His dark and gloomy, Philip Guston-like colors surprisingly summon viewers and activate their minds for unexpected associations (see "Catastrophe").

The idea of a utopian dream, based on wistful, Chekhovian reminiscences, has always interested Oleg Vassiliev. His introspectively nostalgic landscapes are always looking towards some kind of past (be it past experience or past life). A clear illustration of this is his *Home With an Attic*. The very name of the painting reminds the reader of the eponymous Chekhov story. Vassiliev's works are on the borderline between real and unreal, and create a space that is both visual and social. In a unique way, Vassiliev blends the tradition of Russian landscape painting of the end of the nineteenth century and the ideas of the Russian avant-garde of the early twentieth century with its "disregard" for realism, especially the Rayonism of Larionov, the geometrism of Kliun, and the Suprematism of Malevich as well as Italian Futurism. Vassiliev is interested in constructing the space of the picture as closed and finite. His works reveal a regular lyrical meter, broken by the comings and goings of individuals and phenomena. These mystifications of the coming and going of time fused with romantic and symbolic images of the past, and are produced through a hybrid of techniques of Russian post-Impressionism and mystic realism.

The post-modern nostalgia of Vladimir Yankilevsky is nostalgia for the "golden middle" of the departed century, for the postwar years of his childhood. His compositions are subordinated to structural purposes, and the color plays the role of signal emotion. His paintings are constructive and, at the same time, quite emotional. The artist's installation compositions are a pure modernism with elements of eclecticism that convey visual information.

Oleg Vassiliev
From "Home With an Attic" series, 1991 (lithograph, 29 3/4" X 21 1/2", each)

Yankilevsky's descriptive material is like a mask, like a reflection of descriptiveness, but not descriptiveness as such. His installations are architectonic, but this architectonics is ambivalent: it combines a fine form, meant for nuances, with a form coarse, direct, and massive that delivers an apparent visual blow to the viewer. As a whole, it creates an illusion of memory space of postwar Russia and of mass hopes that have to do with that time. The artist skillfully employs Tatlin's device of relief and counter-relief.

Geometric correlations of forms, disruptions, and elements of recognizable objects are developed within the framework of an academic-conceptual tradition. However, the artist's works are broader than this tradition in their creation of a certain plastic-romantic image of either memory or foresight. Having recreated an illusory environment of the communal apartment corridor of his childhood, Yankilevsky attempts to bring this image into the cosmos, thus building an emotional structure of his work based on the art of such Jewish painters as Chagall. This movement upwards into the skies

Natalya Nesterova
Golden Angel, 1999
(oil on canvas, 58" X 52")
Robert and Gloria Cancro Collection

Natalya Nesterova
Angel With Eyes Open, 1991
(oil on canvas, 60" X 48")

from a small Jewish town has, at the same time, a visual connection to classic Pop Art. It is curious that Yankilevsky, being absolutely non-literary in his art, is connected through his emotional roots to the works of such writers as Mikhail Bulgakov and Andrei Belyi, both through his rhythmic modernism (manifested in alternation of figurative and constructive elements) and through his imaginative flights. At the same time, he combines in his series *Take a Train* objects of everyday reality with the biblical, prophesying, paradoxical pathos of Russian literature from Gogol to the Oberiuts. One of the distinctive themes in Yankilevsky's works is engineering: the twentieth century's hope that, in a most interesting way, connects him to literary ideas of Russian modernist writers Boris Pilnyak and Yevgeniy Zamyatin (even though his art is devoid of their more *post*-modern apocalyptic spirit). At the same time, Yankilevsky engages in a dialogue with the ideas of Dos Passos (especially with his *42nd Parallel*) since the artist always combines two visual systems: an emotionality of figures and a schematic constructiveness of elements.

The appearance of the American film *Liquid Sky* by Slava Tsukerman coincided with the rise of neo-expressionism in film as well as the emergence of the Punk movements. Tsukerman drew a parallel between painted faces and extravagant dress proclaimed by the Futurist poet Vladimir Mayakovsky and Futurist artist David Burlyuk (members of the early twentieth-century Russian avant-garde) and the Western Punks of the 1980s. For the director the film was a manifestation of the Russian emigre's nostalgia for the culture of Russia, expressed in the form of nostalgia for Russian Futurism, with echoes of Protazanov's famous film *Aelita*. It was also a more general nostalgia for the ideologically unorthodox (for all such movements were banned in the Soviet Union for decades). Tsukerman also made *Komar and Melamid and Van Gogh*, a film about one of the projects of Vitaly Komar and Alexander Melamid, in which Vincent Van Gogh is regarded as the founder of a religious cult that heals the sick through art. Komar and Melamid play with two cliches here: the cult of Van Gogh and the healing properties of art. The quest for freedom in the unorthodox was further developed with this film, which centers around an emigre artist with an individual artistic language (like Komar and Melamid in America and like Van Gogh was in France).

Michael Odnoralov
Dream, With Pomegranate, 1996
(detail, oil on canvas, 44" X 36")

Semyon Faibisovich has a special role in the development of contemporary Russian art, for he was one of the first to use, along with a photoreporter's emotional distance, those techniques of American Photorealism that were so popular in the US in the 1960s. Despite the highly contemporary nature of his art, Faibisovich's roots go back to the traditions of Russian nineteenth-century realism, which tend toward a matter-of-fact portrayal of life rather than an emphasis on the social aspect of the subject matter. Faibisovich finds the aesthetic in the non-aesthetic, beauty in the banality of everyday life. All of the people he portrays are gloomy, sleepwalking, and absorbed in their own internal world. The artist is externally indifferent to his characters, although his works reveal a distinct social slant. The artist is more interested in an artistic solution than in fostering a social undercurrent. Faibisovich presents reality, leaving the viewer to act as judge if (s)he wishes to do so.

Michael Odnoralov places the heroes of his canvases into the environment of New York's Lower Manhattan. As the buildings draw into themselves, their windows merely reflect light, and the viewer's gaze does not penetrate inside, but instead bounces back from the windows and lands back upon himself. Odnoralov, for his entire artistic career, has been trying to solve the problem of objects in space, objects being metaphysical entities within themselves, and space having an intrinsically ambivalent nature (shifting without effort between various dimensions). It was as part of his investigation of the unruliness of space that Odnoralov arrived at the temple construction. The temple environment is conditionally metaphysical. This very temple construction or temple cone takes its origin in Pavel Florensky's famous philosophical concept of iconostasis. As for the metaphysical realism of Odnoralov's paintings, it is close in spirit to the metaphysical realism of Francis Bacon or Giorgio Morandi, despite all the differences between the latter two. The art, spiritual in its essence, deals with metaphysical issues and not just with pure visual symbols or Surrealism and, within the framework of figurative art, it accomplishes an analysis of the world that is precisely metaphysical. For Odnoralov, this analysis could be traced back to his old passion for philosophy and allows us to trace the development of the artist's philosophical views that were present even in his works of the sixties that, at the first glance, seem so different in terms of artistic style from the series *Alice from the Lower East Side*. The post-modernist compositions of Odnoralov have the same basis as the plastic art of Piet Mondrian. In fact, the early abstract works by Mondrian are abstracted actual three-dimensional landscapes. The same is true for Odnoralov's withdrawal into abstracted environments, in which the essence of an object is revealed much more vividly.

Vitaly Dlugy
Transformation of the Keyhole,
1982
(oil on canvas, 34" X 17")
Robert and Gloria Cancro
Collection

One of the phenomena produced by Natalya Nesterova in her work is to unmask Bakhtin's carnivalesque. Her artistic vision is rooted, in part, in the art of the thirties, as she looked towards artists like Henri Rousseau, Jean Dubuffet and, of course, the Surrealists, (especially Rene Magritte). She did not, however, merely copy the artistic experiments of these painters, in fact the often used them as a starting off point only to go in a completely different conceptual direction. If, for example, Rousseau transformed images into living characters with a personality, Nesterova's creative process moves in the opposite direction; she transforms real personalities into her mystical, tragic, and droll images. Nesterova therein creates her own surreal theater of memories. In her series of paintings *Games on the Beach*, for example, her characters are not just people, but also spaces, objects and insects that were transformed into regalia. The artist examines the realm of human passions by turning living characters into symbols and making them representative of various situations. Quite frequently, Nesterova transforms real characters into images by way of destroying external attributes of their individuality, turning their back to the viewer or positioning them in such a way that the faces of her heroes would be hidden from the viewer. One of the most characteristic devices of transforming Nesterova's characters into images is the act of hiding their faces behind some object or mask. Recently, Nesterova has turned to Jewish themes, seeking their roots in the banality of ordinary life and sensitively observing and registering the mysticism of contemporary life among the Hassid, manifesting an interest in the spiritual development of Jewish culture and refracting it through the theories of the philosopher Martin Buber. The ever-transforming ground of the post-*Perestroika* era has created art that addresses Judaism, and Nesterova is at the forefront of this transformation.

Semyon Faibisovich
In the Subway, 1990
(oil on canvas, 62" X 76")

Vladimir Clavijo-Telepnev
Shukhov Tower, from "Moscow at Night" series, 2003
(photograph, 36" X 29")

The art of Oscar Rabin is an example of Russian post-modernism its eclectic concatenation of forms. The artist uses elements of theoretical studies of Russian art of the twenties combining them with literary traditions of Russian art of the nineteenth century, conceptual art, and elements of Pop Art and kitsch. His art, to a significant degree, follows traditions of the *Peredvizhniki* (Russian Wanderers) of the end of the last century. Rabin uses elements of contemporary modernism, based on which he works out his own artistic-political ideology. His compositions represent a combination of elements that are brought to a unified state and that have the nature of a Pop Art collage, as is the case, for instance, with his "Ashtray". The application to his canvases of various materials, labels, glued slogans, and quoted texts is a purely Pop Art device that Rabin started using, much like other artists of the new avant-garde, while he was still in the former Soviet Union. In Rabin's approach, one can also trace the influence of the Jack of Diamonds group as well as such artists as the early Robert Falk and Peter Konchalovsky (pupils of Valentin Serov and Konstantin Korovin).

Vitaly Dlugy transforms reality into a symbol of philosophic existence, a totem. His totemic system of the world is hierarchical, ranging from the earthy-practical to the celestial-absolute. In his works, each object is transformed into a certain sign - a totemic reflection that carries a memory of the object and of its spiritual essence. Dlugy often juxtaposes the living with the inanimate in his works. He departs from the limits of codified visual modernism creating his own system of recognition and non-recognition of living and non-living objects and as such freely interchanges their functions and identifications. Dlugy can be said, then, to deconstruct living objects. His artistic contemplations texturally revelatory, as they underscore both the expressiveness of movement and the visuality/corporeality of the objects being deconstructed. This process is easily perceived in the *Last Supper* series, where a totally nonfigural composition breaks free of the traditionally emotionless confines of academic still-life, and the constitutive still-life elements of the holy meal act as indexical substitutes for the flesh and blood figures that would have consumed them.

The art of the photographer Naum Kazhdan unpacks the layers of "everyday" reality and reveals its conceptual underpinnings. His photographs are imbued with nostalgia for the lost beauty and spiritual character of Russia. His triptychs appeal to a Renaissance notion of universal aesthetic values, yet at the same time the particular combination/placement of objects in his works challenges the functionality of these classical works of art. The architectonics of space in Kazhdan's work is built on the contrast of large rhythmic forms and concrete details that reveal the meaning and direction of the compositions as a whole. This, to a great degree, determines the form of the triptychs. One sees in his works a contrast of spectral and real, pastoral and violent. Every object is immersed in itself; it is the thing in itself. At the same time, its presence impinges on the existence of the neighboring object. Light and shadow, the rhythmic arrangement of elements, create an atmosphere of anxiety and a certain imbalance of space. Emotional figures, mythological images, and social decorativeness are all expressed in silent conflict.

Genia Chef's works are dominated by the ideology of the wanderer, the cosmopolitan, who both rejects the country of his birth and longs for it. He is an offspring of Bulgakov's understanding of purgatory, of the depths of the fall of the human spirit, the destruction of beauty, and corporeal decay. In the last few years, nostalgia for beauty, for a "paradise lost," has been the basic thrust of this artist's work. His work exists in a typical post-modernist context of intensity and deep subconscious angst. One of his primary creative ideas is of the wanderings of Ahasfer, his travel through Time, whose eternal soul survives dictatorships, wars, and oblivion. Symbolically, he refers to the soul of a Jew, who keeps his skills, knowledge and values through centuries of suffering. In our time, when many artists are becoming universalists who make use of a plethora of styles, artistic trends and stylistic techniques are starting to take on the role of genres. In an era of artistic pluralism, Genia Chef is working in two directions and areas: within a specific multi-style system, combining surrealism with elements of Sots-Art, and with photorealist installations in parallel with computer graphics.

Vladimir Clavijo-Telepnev examines reality within a markedly theatrical context, replete with all of the tragedy and buffoonery of the stage. His art is thus literary (or script-based) by conception. With his theatrical New Romanticism, Clavijo-Telepnev nostalgically sets his post-modern compositions in the settings of times past, re-creating characters that have vanished (David's "Death of Marat" or Ingres' "Girl with a Bird") or creates settings reminiscent of Victorian *tableaux vivants*. Each of his works is like a romantic painting that can exist autonomously, however the obvious quotations in his works are necessarily *re*constructive combinations of nostalgic irony and postmodern analyses of the world.

Having cursorily examined the different artists participating in the "Remembrance" exhibit, the sensible question to now ask is: is there a unifying principle or quality to this group that we tenuously unite under the umbrella of "contemporary Russian art," and if so, what is it? The clearest answer is that what unites the artists in this show is their unanimity with which their creative expressions have been shaped as a direct result of the cultural history they have inherited. This is not to say, of course, that every artist is dealing with precisely the same themes in precisely the same ways. What it does mean, however, is that to dismiss as unrelated the work of two different artists because they use different media or are associated with different artistic schools (or generations, or religions) is to not recognize that be it explicitly or inexplicitly, consciously or not, these artists are working within a shared sociopolitical context and that context shapes in both the finest and grandest ways their individual modes of expression. Interestingly, the effect on their expressive methods of this shared context is has been to develop amongst the various artists in this group an approach to their lives (from past to future) with a spirit that is both forward-looking and nostalgic, relying on past myth as much as future hope, but in the end looking forward (while remembering the past) to a brighter and more freely-expressive future for Russia.

Translated by Lynn Visson and Antonina W. Bouis

RUSSIAN ART FROM PERESTROIKA TO PRESENT • EDWARD LUCIE-SMITH

The history of modernism in Russia dated from the early 1910s. The pre-war and pre-revolutionary years had seen the appearance of innumerable avant-garde groups in St. Petersburg and Moscow, often with wonderfully pictur-esque names – the "Blue Rose," the "Knave of Diamonds," the "Donkey's Tail."

This situation did not endure, for two reasons. One was the increasing hos-tility of the Communist regime towards the activities of experimental artists, which culminated in Stalin's clampdown of 1932-34. In 1932 all liter-ary and artistic organizations were disbanded by decree of the Central Committee of the All-Union Communist Party. In 1934, Socialist Realism was presented as the only viable artistic doctrine at the First All-Union Congress of Soviet Writers. Long before this, however, there had been signs of a loss of energy within the Russian avant-garde itself, and by the late 1920s a great deal of artistic energy was going into parallel activities, espe-cially in to the applied arts and photography. This diversion of aim was not wholly surprising, since Constructivism itself had become increasingly hos-tile to the whole notion of easel-painting, and indeed to the idea of the art-work as a separate entity. The task of the artist was increasingly perceived to be the reshaping and restructuring of the whole social environment.

After the Stalinist clampdown, Russian art inhabited a separate universe from that of Western modernism – or this, at least, was the general percep-tion of artists and critics in the West. The official artists favoured by the Communist regime, rather than looking to the great masters of modernism for inspiration, referred themselves to a specifically Russian tradition, that of the "Itinerants" or "Wanderers" – the group of Realist artists who had flourished in Russia in the late nineteenth and early twentieth centuries. This group included Ivan Kramskoi, Isaac Levitan, and Ilya Repin. Despite the fact that Repin chose to separate himself from the new Russia (he died in exile, in his house just across the Finnish border), his historical scenes, portraits, and politically-oriented genre scenes became the established mod-els for the new Soviet art.

Even after the tide turned against them, some of the surviving members of the original avant-garde who remained in Russia continued to work, but now more or less in secret, and without their original energy and optimism. Malevich, once the most radical of them all, returned to figurative painting in the late 1920s, and his last five years, before his death in 1935, were spent largely on a series of portraits of his friends and members of his immediate family.

The situation for Russian art did not really begin to change until Stalin's death in 1953, and even then change was at first very slow. Russian art, which had for more than twenty years been almost completely cut off from artistic developments in the West, began to have intermittent contact with what was going on outside its own country. One major stimulus was the Sixth World Festival of Youth and Students held in Moscow in the summer of 1957. A feature of this was an enormous exhibition – over 4,500 works – of painting and sculpture by young artists from 52 countries. One result was the appearance of the Soviet unofficial art movement. Towards the end of the 1950s certain artists began to hold private exhibitions in the homes of sympathetic members of the Russian intelligentsia, and these were followed by others held in scientific research institutes and various club premises. The movement surfaced in public in 1962, when a number of paintings and sculptures by younger and more experimental members of the

Artists' Union (the official organization which embraced all forms of artistic activity) were included in a large exhibition held to mark the thirtieth anniversary of the Union's Moscow section. This exhibition was held in the city's biggest exhibition hall, the ManŹge, and triggered a furious tirade from its most important visitor, the Party chairman, Nikita Khrushchev.

The unofficial movement continued into the 1970s, and attracted wide publicity through exhibitions organized on an ad hoc basis. The first of these, held on a patch of waste land near Moscow in September 1972, was attacked by police disguised as workers. Paintings were thrown into dump-trucks or run over by bulldozers, and a number of participants and specta-

tors were arrested. The violence was counterproductive from the point of view of the authorities, since Western journalists had been in attendance, and what happened was widely reported in the Western press. Examples of the new art began to find their way out of Russia, and in January 1977 a large representative exhibition opened at the Institute of Contemporary Arts in London. Similar exhibitions were also seen elsewhere.

The story of the return of Russian art and Russian artists to the contemporary scene is best told, not in simplistic terms of a rebellion against the Soviet establishment, which in the end succeeded, but in those of the gradual, then more rapid, changes affecting Soviet society in the post-Stalin years, which eventually led to the collapse of the Soviet Union itself. The Russian art which now ranks as "contemporary" is in many ways more intimately linked to the tradition of Socialist Realism than it is to that of the original Russian avant-garde. An artists like Oleg Kudriashov is very much a maverick in terms of the new Russian art, because his work is abstract, and does relate to the history of constructivism of the Russian Revolutionary epoch – to Tatlin's classic *Corner Reliefs* in particular.

The changes in Soviet art which took place after the death of Stalin involved a gradual reinterpretation of Socialist Realist doctrine. Official artists like Evsei Moiseenko adopted a looser, somewhat more romantic style, while making use of approved precedents in the Soviet past. Moiseenko's work derives from the work of the Petersburg Symbolist, and former member of the Blue Rose group, Kuzma Petrov-Vodkin, who afterwards threw in his lot with the Revolution. Petrov-Vodkin's Death of the Commissar, painted in 1928, became one of the best-loved icons of Soviet art. Another Soviet academician, Dmitri Zhilinski, produced work which was heavily influenced by traditional icon painting – the religious connotations of these were forgiven because of the impeccable "Russianness" of the source. Another factor for change in the art of the late Soviet period was a gradual return to a style which has never been automatically associated with Russia in the West – figurative Expressionism. For Russian artists, the chief exemplar for this style was Alexandr Drevin, persecuted under Stalin for his refusal to conform. It is Drevin's influence which can be detected in the work of practitioners of the so-called "Severe Style" of official art.

These experiments indicated that the boundaries for artists were being loosened. What they did not in the end indicate was the precise direction which the new Russian art would take. A much clearer indication of this came from the work and careers of Vitaly Komar and Alexsander Melamid. Trained in the Russian tradition of official art, these two artists began their collaboration in 1972, painting a mural for the Alley of Heroes at a Young Pioneers summer camp. In the early and mid-1970s they were much involved in the activities of the nascent group of dissident artists in Moscow, participating both in the outdoor exhibition which was broken up by the authorities, and in a subsequent outdoor show at Izmailovsky Park which had an enormous impact on the public. In 1976 they held their first exhibition in New York, which was also the fist public showing of what a friend of theirs had already labeled "Sots-Art" – the Soviet version of Pop. The artists liked the term and it stuck, though it gives a somewhat false impression of what they do. Far from celebrating mass culture, as Pop Art does, their work seeks to deconstruct an official culture imposed from above. In 1978 the duo emigrated to the United States, where they have lived and worked ever since.

What made Komar and Melamid famous was the skill with which they parodied the Soviet official style at its most kitsch. The satire is at its most telling in a series of paintings devoted to the official cult of Stalin. In *The Origins of Socialist Realism*, the dictator is inspired by a partly nude muse, who chucks him lovingly under the chin. The style is Davidian classicism at its most grandiose. In the Western world the paintings appealed because they allowed the audience to have its cake and ear it – to enjoy the traditional skills of the artists while at the same time relishing the ironic comedy of the imagery. In Russia, this and similar work had a much more complex resonance. Both in their daily lives, and in dealing with the censored but often quietly rebellious forms of artistic expression the authorities allowed them to enjoy – books and films were more generally accessible in this respect than paintings and other works of visual art – Russian audiences were well accustomed to unraveling codes and reading subtexts. As the regime began to liberalize itself, artists began to turn its own characteristic imagery against it.

The paintings of Eric Bulatov, in particular, chronicle the decline and fall of Soviet Russia through images carefully culled form the standard Soviet repertoire, built up over many years – under Stalin and his immediate successors, and finally under Brezhnev. Bulatov adopts different strategies in different compositions. *Perestroika* turns the established imagery of the regime, and even its standard typographical forms, against itself. The two hands, one holding a hammer and the other a sickle, which are the focus of the composition, are a quotation, instantly recognizable to any Russian, from a famous sculptural group by the Socialist Realist sculptor Vera Mukhina, representing a worker and a collective farm girl. This group, made in 1937 at the height of Stalin's purges, has been described ironically as "the Soviet Statue of Liberty."

Other leading Russian artists of the *Perestroika* epoch have been concerned with more rarefied forms of cultural analysis. Svetlana Kopystiansky works with literary texts, using them as the basis for assemblages, often of ambitious scale. Ilya Kabakov also makes much use of texts, usually indecipherable to the Western audience, but his popularity is due to the emotional accessibility of his work. Kabakov evokes the realities of late Soviet and post-Soviet society: the hypocrisy, the decay of institutions, the daily struggle to survive, but at the same time celebrates the resilience of the human spirit in the face of so many frustrations and privations. The constructivists who sided with the Revolution looked forward to an utopian future. For Kabakov an optimism of this kind is no longer possible.

While they see the remnants of the academic system of art training set up by the Soviets as a precious legacy which ought to be preserved rather than dismantled in the name of a new era of political freedom, members of the Novia Akademia such as, for example, Genia Chef, also experiment boldly with new techniques, including computer digitilisation and alteration of photographic images. The real reference pointy for the Novia Akademia is, however, not the Stalinist era but the period just before the fall of the tsars. Chef uses the computer to create works which have and eerie resemblance to the art of the past, but which yet, in many respects, remain visibly and substantially different.

1 Matthew Cullerne Brown, Contemporary Russian Art, Oxford, 1989, p.31.
2 Artist's statement in The Quest for Self-Expression: Painting in Moscow and Leningrad, 1965-1990 (exh. Cat.), Columbus Museum of Art, Columbus, Ohio, 1990, p. 108.
3 Matthew Cullerne Brown, op. cit., pp. 78-81.

IDENTITY FORMATION IN THE POST-SOVIET STATE • DONALD KUSPIT

Komar & Melamid
Scenes From the Future:
Museum of Modern Art, c. 1992
(lithograph, 24" X 30")

This exhibition touches every base of Russian art since the sixties, beginning with the modernist art of that time, and ending with the current development of post-modern eclecticism. The latter looks backward to the seminal art of Russian constructivism, and forward to deconstructivism, fusing these opposites in an attempt to give new meaning to art at a time when it has become overloaded with self consciousness - for some, a sign of decadence. To approach the artists in terms of their stylistic differences is beside the point; the diversity of their styles reflects that of the twentieth century itself - a time of restless change and dissatisfaction with the status quo - and suggests that there is no consistent, ideal model of art, but a number of equally valid modes of art-making. Thus stands the eclecticism that appropriates many of them. One has only to look at Michael Odnoralov's complicated, subtle paintings - a strange union of beauty and irony - to see the point: a mix of figuration (the naked bodies), constructivism (the abstract

Komar & Melamid
*Scenes From the Future:
Guggenheim Museum*, c. 1992
(lithograph, 24" X 30")

planes), and Social Realism (the urban buildings). They are impossible to categorize. The ingenious synthesis of discrepant elements - the friction yet the attraction between them - is powerfully evocative. But the best one can do is to try to decipher the expressive riddle of the work, which draws one to it, with the hope of gaining insight into the mind that produced it.

That is what I will try to do: articulate the state of mind signaled by the works. I want to argue that however wide-ranging they are, they have something obvious in common; they are all produced by Russians, and all respond, however obliquely, to the difficulties of existence in Soviet Russia, difficulties which have left their mark on post-Soviet Russia.

I submit that the problem of achieving an autonomous identity and strong sense of selfhood haunts the Russian art in this exhibition, and that it

Natalya Nesterova
*Dream on the Shore
(Reading Buber)*, 1999
(oil on canvas, 50" X 56")

achieves such identity and selfhood by standing in rebellious, ironical relationship to the Soviet past, whether signaled through style or iconography.
The point is to achieve a very un-Soviet expressivity and meaning even
when using the paraphernalia of Soviet style. This is in essence what Komar
and Melamid do in their *Nostalgic Socialist Realism* series. Alexander the
Great, 1983, is a nasty spoof on tyranny - Alexander substituting for the
Soviet dictator - carried out with a post-modern mix of means in which
every element is deconstructed into double, self-contradictory meaning. The
portrait bust of Alexander is both a work of high ancient art and a kitsch
quotation, just as the gestural drips and flat non-illusionistic ground have
become the cliches of American abstract expressionism and field painting.
Standard elements responsible for "the triumph of American (abstract) art"
as well as a symbol of the authority of the state - delusions of artistic and
social grandeur - are simultaneously fused and mocked. The anarchistic
humor of the painting is indicated by the schematic arms and legs added to
the figure, turns it into a cartoon—a perverse joke. Komar and Melamid's
"Anarchistic Synthecism," to refer to the title of the series, is a determined
effort to deny all authority, artistic and social, which claims absolute power
over the individual. Their anarchistic and contrarian imagination is a rebellion against any and every system of hegemony.

The non-conformist rebellion of Vitaly Dlugy, Natalya Nesterova, and
Oscar Rabin consists in their turning to modernist style, intimate studio
themes, and spiritualist imagery, as though to thwart the Soviet credo that
the only significant life one has is the one that belongs to the state - the
life that officially and publicly existed. The fluid, spontaneous, expressionist handling evident in the paintings of Dlugy and Rabin countermands the

predictable handling demanded by Socialist Realism. Nesterova's revival of Jewish themes, conceived of as primitive theatrical performances, which makes them all the more eerie in the context of Soviet society, is an open affront to Soviet anti-religious ideology. The still life themes - in effect still life dramas - of Dlugy and Rabin are also radically inward. They suggest a private sanctuary where intense emotional expression is possible - a space altogether antithetical to Soviet public space, where one must remain inexpressive, or respond in a fixed way according to social expectations. The new Soviet man was as other-directed as any American suburbanite, and the intimate character and introspective qualities of the neo-spiritual art in this exhibition is in direct rebellion against such programmed other-directedness. Where Komar and Melamid take the ironical sociopolitical route in their rebellion against Soviet society and dogma, the neo-spiritual artists turn inward to escape it. Which is more progressive, which more regressive - humanly as well as artistically - is hard to say these post-modern days, when all stylistic and expressive means are at the artist's disposal?

Vladmir Yankilevsky has chosen the path of conceptual-aesthetic revolt against Soviet artistic rule. The enigmatic iconography of Yankilevsky's Train series has a surrealist flavor. Ordinary objects are "analyzed" into planar sections, which are then reconstructed into abstract images that seem altogether autonomous. Nothing is stable in these works; indeed, their vertigo and fragmentation suggest the dizzying freedom and uncertain spontaneity of post-Soviet artistic possibilities. A similar fragmentation is evident in Odnoralov's works, and a similar haunting sense of incompleteness in their composition, conveying a feeling of fatalism for all the freshness of the young naked bodies.

Although I have argued that the works in this exhibition are a response to the Soviet conception of art, they nonetheless have their place in the larger history of post-modern art. Every one of them is an expressive hybrid of avant-garde ideas, whatever their sociopolitical implications. There is a sense of reprise - Rabin's works are a remarkable synthesis of Cubist and Expressionist ideas, Dlugy's turbulent imagery is an important contribution to Expressionism, Komar and Melamid use both traditional imagery and modernist methods. By definition, the individual is unique, and yet all these works seem to have a certain kind of common individuality, whatever their differences: out of their opposition to the Soviet status quo, the artists have forged a sense of forces in perpetual opposition. The ironists as well as the spiritualists are equally combative, and leave us with a sense that harmony is impossible.

Comprehensive intelligibility is never achieved, in part because it is impossible to make sense of the Soviet system, in part because, with its collapse, he has been thrown into art history, with its confusing options. Lacking any models of authentic social and artistic harmony, the contemporary Russian artist can only labor on his or her contradictions in hopes of making sense of his or her experience. Even the religionists among the artists, who might seem to have made their transcendental escape successfully, are stuck with the absurdity of believing in myths that have been as discredited as the Soviet myth of the new society. Disillusionment permeates all of this art and so it cannot find peace with itself.

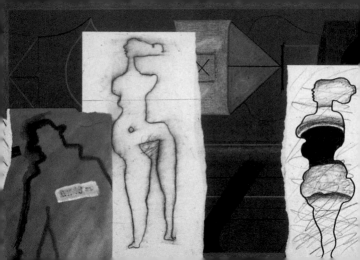

THE PULVERIZATION OF THE BLACK SQUARE • SONYA ABADIYEVA

Kazimir Malevich started his new painting in Europe from point zero. In 1915, his scenographic drawing for the play "Victory" promoted the abstract essence of the black square. Regardless of whether he was aware of the bright future of the black square, and of his own art, the square became a symbol of the beginning and the end - from the stone age to the airplane, from pagan times through Christianity and the black cubic building that is Mecca's Ka'ba.

Malevich's square has since burst into dozens of pieces. The compact geometric structure anticipated in its very constitution the concept of (its own) catastrophe, providing a conceptual foundation for two driving forces in Russian art that followed: deconstruction and antagonism. In addition to opening a path for deconstructive and antagonistic artwork, Malevich also put forward the relevance of quasi-atavistic emotionality ("Man was born to be excited") and thus completed the motivational triumvirate of contemporary Russian art.

The concept of catastrophe connects us to "The Island of Death" by the German classicist Arnold Bucklin, forbidden by Lenin and adored by Hitler, (and one of the painter Genia Chef's favorite paintings, as well). It is known that there were such islands of death in a number of ex-socialist countries (Goli Otok in former Yugoslavia was created after World War II). In the former Soviet Union, during the rule of Iosif Visarionovich Dzhugashvili Stalin, the spirit of catastrophe burst into all the areas of life including art. The creative force of the artists of the Russian vanguard was squeezed into the square of the compulsory, unique and absolute stylistic form called Socialist Realism: the aestheticism (aisthetike) transferred to anesthesia (an-aisthesis), i.e. emotion as a lexical base of aesthetics was reduced to insensitivity, but not numbness.

The pulverization of the Black Square turned into reality on all ontological levels: it deprived the artist of the freedom of expression - his holiest and apodictically the most significant component. Repressions, bans, censures, wire-tappings, denunciations, arrests and loyalty to the leader and his ideol-

Victory Over the Sun – futurist opera
Created by Malevich/Kruchonykh/Matyushin in 1913 in St. Petersburg.
Recreated (photo) by Dreznin/Kaufman/Karlbauer in 1993 with debut in Vienna, Austria

ogy contaminated the countries of the Warsaw Pact as well: Poland, Romania, Bulgaria, Hungary, Czechoslovakia, East Germany, and Yugoslavia. The despotism of Socialist Realism, as a collective code, proved the incongruity with the personal articulation of the artist and repressed the identity or reduced it to a double identity. In the second case, Narcissus turned into Janus. The dilemma posed by a "Who Am I?" left psychological, sociological, cultural and artistic scars.

Traces of the repression of totalitarian regimes in the former Soviet Union were not equally deep in all of the aforementioned countries. The artists in Poland and Czechoslovakia were carefully and continuously getting out of the ghetto of Socialist Realism exploring the opportunities of Expressionism, Cubism, and geometrical abstraction. A special case was the union of the Yugoslav peoples (now peoples with independent entity: Serbia and Montenegro, Bosnia and Herzegovina, Slovenia, Macedonia and Croatia). During a short period of time, during and after World War II, the whole culture bore the symbol of this type of realism. After the Information Bureau (1948) and Marshal Tito said his historic "NO" to Stalin, the situation started to soften. But in 1952 (during the Congress of Writers), the erudite, encyclopaedist and writer Miroslav Krleza opened up the road to free artistic expression. For the sake of truth, intellectuals were being arrested and deported to Goli Otok afterwards as well. This occurred simultaneously with the establishment of the New Tendencies and Conceptualism, especially in Croatia and Serbia, and of the vanguard group Denes (Today) (1953) in Macedonia, influenced by the Russian vanguard, De Stijl, Bauhaus, and Fluxus. But it is a fact that in former Yugoslavia, and in some other Eastern Bloc countries and regions, the artists respected their own as well as world tradition in parallel with their admiration for the Russian art of the 1920s (Mladen Stilinovich, Vlado Martek, the IRWIN group, Rasa Todosijevich, Jovan Sumkovski, Aleksandar Stankovski, Vlado Gotovac, Braco Dimitrijevich, Dusan Percinkov, and Dragan Petkovich). Some of them, with graded irony, reinterpreted the work of Russian vanguard artists and the socialist leaders and heroes, but lacked a strict and sharp critical approach to the socialist system.

In some of their concepts, sometimes humorously referred to as "Exploitation of the Dead" (Mladen Stilinovich), the genuine beginnings of modernism were being recognized (although sometimes ridiculed too). However, they were insignificant compared to the excessive amount of adrenalin (apodictic sarcasm, merciless parody, anger and resistance) deposited in the works of their Russian colleagues of the Soviet underground stage before the *Perestroika* and *Glasnost,* and even afterwards (Ilya Kabakov, Michail Chemyshev, Dmitri Prigov, Komar & Melamid, the groups, the magazines, the exhibitions, the performances and the movements, the styles: Mukhomor, The Nest, Conceptual Seminar, A/YA Magazine, ARTART, Collective Actions, Sukharevsky Exhibition, Bulldozer Action, theCMoscow conceptual art, ARTART, etc.). Balint Szombathy and Janos Sugar from Hungary, Simon Shemov and the group Zero from Macedonia, Rasa Todosijevich and Marina Abramovich from Serbia, Braco Dimitrijevich and the group Zvono from Bosnia and Herzegovina, Ion Grigorescu from Romania, Mangelos, Stilinovich, Tomislav Gotovac and Martek from Croatia, Jiri Kovanda from Czechoslovakia, The Ljubljana Lacan School, the groups Laibach, V.S.S.D, NSK and IRWIN from Slovenia, the exhibition Kazimir Malevich (reconstructed fiction realized in Belgrade), Lyuben

Komar & Melamid
Alexander the Great,
from "Nostalgic
Socialist Realism" series, 1983
(oil on canvas, 72" X 48")

Kostov, Svetlin Roussev and the group The City from Bulgaria, worked under the influence of these phenomena or in synchrony with them.

The cells holding fine arts in the Soviet Union in the age of their anesthesia (more than two decades long) gradually released their creative energy in the 1960s and the 1970s. Out of a coma, they went out to capture the world as a new Russian paradigm in the 1980s and the 1990s coincided with the tragedy of emigration of the most important representatives (largely to the US, France and Germany).

These artists-emigrants became bi-patriates. The phenomenon of belonging to two countries is of essential significance for all artists-emigrants and for Russians in particular. As people brought up in the isolation of the system and far behind what was going on in the meantime in the world of modernism, craving to overcome the mortgage of the past, they plunged into the post-modernistic fields in the most sincere and justified manner. It is from here that a pronounced eclecticism sprang out, which is attributed to the Russian art of today, and which they very adeptly manipulate. The distinctive feature of their post-historic empirics was rooted in the integration of the adopted foreign discourses with melancholy and nostalgia and with the connotations adopted from the Russian tradition of the past: the folklore, the icon-painting, the symbols of the totalitarian regime (the leaders, the heroes and their monuments/mausoleums, the hammer and sickle, the red star and the red color). The wish to be there (in another world) and the wish not to lose the features of a national identity sparkled feelings of explicit antagonisms in their largely figurative works. On the other hand, however contradictory it seems, both their own icons and the artistic icons of capitalism (Warhol's Pop Art, Pollock's dripping procedure) turned into the main target of their deconstructive practices. The anger and resistance of the artists, which had accumulated for decades, became stereotyped and cliché (whatever the provenance), and was being expressed in the act of that destruction with abundant doses of irony, sarcasm and parody. The highly emotional reactions in this sense of Komar & Melamid, Ilya Kabakov, Mikhail Roginsky or Leonid Sokov were and still are the bases of the Russian ontological artistic particularity. Let me quote Malevich once again: "Man was born to be excited".

The ecstasy of cynicism reached its paroxysm in the "Red Pavilion" – Ilya Kabakov's masterpiece – "mounted" at the Venetian Giardini in 1993, as an exclusive presentation of Russia at the International biennial. Created in a Lilliputian version, studded with all the symbols of the former Soviet Union (red flags, small and big five-pointed stars and the national coat of arms), this pavilion alongside the bitter sarcasm, expressed the admirable humor of eminent Russian writers, such as Esop, Gogol, Voynovich and Bulgakov.

Grisha Bruskin (above)
Flaming Angel, from "Metamorphoses" series, 1992
(enamel on steel, 30" X 15" X 9")

Grisha Bruskin (left)
Visage, from "Metamorphoses" series, 1992
(enamel on steel, 21" X 9 3/8" X 9")

Jovan Balov,
Me and You, 2001
(acrylic and print
on canvas)

In the painting of Komar & Melamid in which a beautiful girl from some
bygone time gently caresses Stalin, the irony flavored with grotesque is ter-
rifying. If you take into consideration the paintings of the cycle *Nostalgic
Socialist Realism of 1983* "Alexander the Great" and "Discobolus" by the
same authors, you realize that Jackson Pollock and antiquity nullify one
another, indicating both symbolically and realistically the end of the invio-
lable values sealed in the history of art as eternity. In this regard, these
artists are closely related to the Croatian Conceptualists Vlado Martek, M.
Stilinovic, T. Gotovac, the Serbian artists R. Todosijevich and Marina
Abramovic (now in the US) and the Macedonian artists A. Stankovski and
Jovan Balov. The humor/irony is slightly softer in the work of the Czech
Cherny David, the Bulgarian Luchezar Boyadijev and the IRWIN group from
Slovenia. The not so aggressive variants of the clash with the conformism of
the Russian authors Natalya Nesterova, Larisa Zvezdochotova, Konstantin
Zvezdochotov, Rimma Gerlovina, Valery Gerlovin may be related (in under-
standably different visual and conceptual expression) to the installations of
B. Dimitrievich (expatriate) from Bosnia and Herzegovina, Elizabeta
Avramovska, Zaneta Vangeli and Dushan Percinkov from Macedonia, Dan
Perjovischi from Romania or Nedko Solakov from Bulgaria.

The exploitation of the dead, and now of the living artists as well, created
yet another characteristic of contemporary Russian art: necro-realism. Its
founding father, the film-maker Eugeny Yufit, with a group of painters in
1984 in Saint Petersburg (former Leningrad), in search of the reality of
death, broke into the areas of the ultimate "insensitivity, ecstasy and the
corporeal". Inspired by the psychiatric literature, Yufit's films are depressive
to excess and reduced reality to corpses and decay as much as they forayed
into the metaphysical and the mystical. Their nihilism (the Punk movement
being a counterpart) expressed itself with necrophilic ferocity bred, among
other things, on the works of Nietzsche, Cioran, and Schopenhauer. The elements of self-hurting bring some performances and installations by M.
Abramovich and Iskra Dimitrova (from Macedonia) close to the eschatological type.

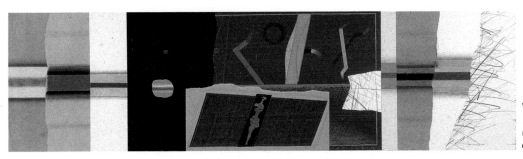

Vladimir Yankilevsky
Train 2, from "City" series, 1992
(pastel, gouache, pencil, and
collage on cardboard, 25" X 76")

Group "Trio": Dalila Durakovic, Bojan Hadzihalilovic and Leila Mulabegovic
Coca-Cola - Sarajevo, 1993
(tempera on paper)

The output of the participants of the New Academy movement has been created in a completely different fashion and rests on a different system, speaking of transience and relativity in more complex ways. Genia Chef (today an active artist mainly in the Berlin artistic scene) is the promoter of this Academy. He speaks about the "new Russian dance of death". The "scenography" of his works (dioramas, photographs, paintings, plotters) is tendentiously ambivalent blending antiquity, the Renaissance and classicism, and the secession within the ruins of the past in which a living being wanders troubled by philosophical questions in the Berlin subway. The paradox occurs at the level of the inversion of the real and the meta-

Tomislav Gotovac,
Sickle, Hammer and Red Star,
1984, performance

Ion Grigoescu
Dialog with Comrade Causescu, 1975-1991
(instalation)

Milomir Kovachevic
Tito - Sarayevo, 1992-1995
(photograph)

physical: what is physically dead as a product of the hand of the creators
in the history of art (the ancient and classical sculptures and paintings)
carries the aura and freshness of the living and contrasts with the biolog-
ical reality of the man (in the subway) who roams like an imagined ghost
in G. Chef's imaginary museum. Death confronted with the ontological,
and beauty confronted with ugliness, conspire a holistic system, and
bring back the dialogue over relativity. But the ultimate impression this
author creates is the melancholic longing for the lost harmony. Isn't this
a craving for aestheticism (aisthetike) in the classical sense following the
definite liberation from the decades-long anesthesia (an-aisthesia) in the
Russian fine arts? The above-mentioned features of the modern Russian
artistic articulations reveal the necessity of introducing a new terminolo-
gy in the fine arts, as well as restructuring, reinterpreting and reevalu-
ating the reigning hierarchy of values. At present, this is done with very
phlegmatic rhythm and with strict selectiveness by the arbiters of art. I
believe that today Russian art draws from the ground of identity or
idiosyncrasy and refuses to renounce the project that characterizes
modernism. It is on its way to reach the heights from which European
modernism set out in the age of the Russian vanguard of the twentieth
century.

Translated by Alexandra Ilievska

FROM METAPHORS OF ALIENATION • KATHRIN BECKER

Contemporary Russia is facing a problem connected to the fact that it still had not been able to develop in its own milieu a new definition for the concept of "culture."1 The concept of Russian modernism (i.e., the classical Russian and Soviet avant-garde of the 1910s and 1920s) was replaced in the early 1930s by the concept of Socialist Realism, which subsumed artistic expression under the political ideals and programs of the state. The task of artists was to match the needs of the Party to those of the socialist society. Socialist Realism rejected the idea of individual identity, with a single principle of consciousness stemming from an "I." Actually, it tried to erase the "I" and substitute a "We." The claim was to achieve a complete concurrence of the needs of the individual and those of society, in effect a resolution of the contradiction of the modern condition that pits the individual against society. In this context, the needs of the individual, when they differed from those that the Party identified for society, were not only thought to be futile, but were also interpreted as hostile to the building of a true socialist society.

In the transition from Marxism-Leninism to Stalinism, the definition of cultural identity underwent a sharp turn: "world revolution" and the related overcoming of national identity gave way in the 1930s to Stalin's idea of "socialism in one country." The thesis contains an elevation of the nation, and in this particular case within the context of Soviet patriotism. In art, Stalinization meant a turn to the familiar themes of The Homeland and The People. Cast aside during the Revolution, the concept of national cultural identity made a comeback. It is in this context that the campaign against formalism in the 1930s demanded a return to Russian national cultural heritage. In the figurative arts for instance, this produced artwork reminiscent of the 19th-century Russian realists - the so-called Wanderers (*Peredvizhniki*).

The division of Soviet cultural space in the 1960s into two spheres, official and unofficial, corresponds to the formation of two opposite forms of identity. One was distinguished by a systemic conformity and loyalty to the idea of the socialist state. The other, based primarily on (Western) modernist ideas, stood for the "freedom of art" as an expression of the freedom of the individual. However, both camps had to locate themselves vis-a-vis the continued existence of socialism, either pro or con.

With the implementation of reforms initiated under Mikhail Gorbachev (*Perestroika*), the terms of the contradiction were blurred. Socialist Realism lost its significance as a result of these reforms that allowed for both the differentiation of the function of art in society and the expression of the artist as an individual.

Naturally, official criticism and theory of art did not pay much attention to the analysis of nonconformist works in Soviet art (see Eric Bulatov), and as a result, were unable to set guidelines for the elaboration of new cultural policy directives; criteria for a new, universally recognized artform that corresponded to the self-expression and representation needs of the reformed state.

The West had a decisive influence on the appreciation of cultural developments in Russia. Interest in defeating socialism in Eastern Europe made the support and study of formerly "unofficial art" an important aspect of foreign cultural policy of many Western European countries. Starting in the

Genia Chef
In the Valley of the Giants, 2003
(digital print, light box in
three dimensions,
15 3/4" X 31 1/2" X 2 1/3")

late 1980s, museums held large review exhibits of Muscovite art. These initiatives eventually turned into a focused promotion of one specific tendency in the course of its development: Moscow Conceptualism, epitomized by the work of Ilya Kabakov.

Nowadays, Moscow Conceptualism is the most important commodity in contemporary Russian art. This peculiar distribution of Russian art in the West was facilitated by a series of favorable circumstances of which Ilya Kabakov's works of the 1990s offer a good illustration. Moscow Conceptualism with its ontological character was able to reflect the details of Soviet daily life in a way that fortified the West in its own ideological outlook. The hell of the Soviet communal apartment, with its kitchen and toilet, evidences to the Western viewer, who has his own domestic comfort in mind, the impossibility of dignified human existence in a planned economy. Moreover, Moscow Conceptualism operates with the same blurring methods of integrating context in a work of art that (and here lies the paradox) guarantee its compatibility with various forms of the manifestation of Concept-Art. In Moscow Conceptualism (and in Sots-Art of Komar and Melamid, Kosolapov, and Sokov), just as in certain directions of American postwar art (Pop Art), anthropology takes the forefront as a stylistic method and eventually becomes the normative style.

In a certain sense, the success of Moscow Conceptualism is as an indicator of the acceptance of the cultural ideology of the victor, that is, capitalism. However, this applies only to cultural exports, and cannot necessarily be assigned to conceptualist art from everywhere in Eastern Europe (see Manovtseva and Shuravlev). As for Russia itself, the works of Ilya Kabakov remain essentially unknown. Reflecting the future in a sense through the past, it is addressing an ideology that is now alien. It is, on the one hand ill-equipped to satisfy the political demands of the cultural self-expression of the new Russia and, on the other, incapable of developing its own cultural self-definition.

Sasha Manovtseva
Russian Tongue (Triptych), 2001
(color photograph, 20" X 34")
Aaron Katz Collection

Sasha Manovtseva
Lemon (Triptych), 2001
(color photograph, 18" X 34")

Eric Bulatov
Go, Stop, Go, 1973
(pencil and ink on paper, 15" X 15")
Yuri and Nelly Traisman Collection

Eric Bulatov
Perestroika, 1989
(lithograph, 18" X 18")
Yuri and Nelly Traisman Collection

With the collapse of the eastern bloc, Western Europe felt it incumbent on itself to help the Eastern European countries find and define their national identity. This took place within the framework of supporting the idea of particularism. The concept of a "Europe of Regions" was elaborated to fit the conjuncture. Western Europe saw the emerging situation in terms of its own experience post-World War II. This fostered the accelerated development of nationalism in the states of the former USSR (and Eastern Europe as a whole).

In this context, Germany had missed the chance that appeared after 1945 to give a new definition for the concept of "culture." The starting point ("zero hour") in West Germany came at time of desire for primacy for the concept of modernism. However, its contradictions never did become the subject of analysis and discussion. An example of this is the adherence of modernism to the principles of internationalism, universalism, and totality without a critical reappraisal of its attitude toward the "primitive," the savage, and the female among other things. Even the Frankfurt school asked whether the totality and universalism characteristic of modernism were building blocks of totalitarianism. In the post-modern period, some of the concepts of modernism became subject to criticism and revision. The only result, however, is the tendency to substitute post-modern particularism for modernist totality as a cultural directive. For the states of the former Soviet Union, this means that the process of changing the obsolete socialist ideology took place under the sign of the idea of liberation from totalitarianism and a return to national values. This nationalism could be called differentiating nationalism,

Rimma Gerlovina &
Valeriy Gerlovin
Heaven/Hell, 1989
(Ectacolor print, 36" X 36")

as opposed to Soviet patriotism, which had defined everything national first of all in relation to the union of nations in which specific national traits of individual ethnicities were subjugated to the Russian cultural heritage, Russian language, and Russian written culture. The new republics manifest a desire for a return to their status before becoming part of the Soviet Union, a desire to eradicate traces of the Soviet period from their history. The formation of a collective identity out of the "sum of historical memories about one's own political actions" (Werner Weidenfeld) leads in this context to a vision skewed toward national values. Thus, identity is in a "differentiated non-antagonistic relationship with all other identities" and "has as its precondition not only the existence of all other identities but also the preconditions creating their differences per se."2 This means that the new relations arising among (national) groups aim at oppressing an "other."

Anatoly Shuravlev
Tattoo, 1995
(c-paint, 57" X 40")

Contemporary Russia faces the question of the ideological function of art in society. These questions are investigated by such artists as Anatoly Shuravlev and Sasha Manovtseva. As mentioned above, the specifics of the export of contemporary Russian art are heavily determined by the West and are subject to the laws of the Western art market (as in the case of the Gerlovins). However, this fact, relying on Western demand, does not answer the question about the future of art production in Russia. The cultural exchange between Western Europe and Russia creates a false picture of the situation inside the country: the projects and exhibits in Western Europe satisfy first the desire of the West to achieve primacy in the East vis-a-vis its own expression of modernism. The exhibits of contemporary Russian art in the West say little about the situation in the country. As much as the rules of particularism in cultural politics extend to art itself, we can recognize the existence of a hierarchy of structures based on the significance of the organizations that are the bearers of culture in society.3 Exhibition activity is self-reflexive and intended only to reflect events taking place in Western European cultural institutions. The practice of exhibition in Russia is totally unknown in the West. From my point of view, cultural exchange between the West and the East contains more information about Western European problems than the culture to which it is allegedly devoted. A comparison of cultures could have made possible not only an analysis of what has already taken place but also of what might have taken place.

Translated by Antonina W. Bouis

1 The discussion published here on the issues of a new definition of culture in Russia are based on the text of Peter Weibel's article, "Probleme der Neomoderne," in Peter Weibel / Christa Steinle, Hrsg, Identitat Differenz. Graz, 1992, pp. 3-21.
2 Ernesto Laclau, Universalitat, Partikularismus und die Frage der Identitat, in Peter Weibel / Christa Steinle, op. cit.
3 Peter Weibel sees a hierarchical structure of the domination of Americanocentrism over Eurocentrism in Eastern Europe.

ASPECTS OF RENEWAL: RUSSIAN ODYSSEYS • ALEXANDER BOROVSKY

The representation of any art, and a fortiori that of Russian and Russian-born artists, is a process inevitably fraught with stereotypes: a gentleman's collection of names, forms, and phenomena, some formidable hierarchies, and a stepping over that seems to be breaking the rules of the game. In a word, it is like the name of that old Soviet film, "Foreigners are not welcome."

For this reason, one cannot but welcome any attempt that helps refresh our perception of this material. This is the task that Alexandre Gertsman takes on as curator. The sharpening of the perception occurs by adding new names, and by bringing out unexpected and exact ties between artists who have long ago announced themselves on the art stage. Seamlessly, a real exhibition unites artists from different generations, different levels of fame, and different media installations.

Topping this already important contribution, artists, including veterans, are presented as ever developing through their new work. This is a pleasure because, sadly, the practice in the contemporary art scene is such that many masters, having reached a certain level of success, prefer not to "rock the boat," but simply continue to produce what is expected of them, and thus reinforce the notions that the public has already formed about their art. As the philosopher M. Gasparov wrote about one famous poet: "from a semantic point of view he was a symbol of himself."

In this regard, it seems that the principle behind this exhibition is less the symbols and more the living.

Such is the approach of presenting the artists who entered the art stage as far back as the 60's. In Russia they were called *Shestidesyatniki*, and this term suggests a whole complex of political, socio-cultural, in reality cultural understandings, a "common denominator" of which turned out to be a daunting, but inevitable process to acquire inner freedom. The next generation will concentrate on new aesthetic dilemmas, but this feeling of freedom they will take as a given - thanks to the work of the *Shestidesyatniki*. Perhaps for the first time after the 1920s, after the prohibition of artistic gatherings, they asserted themselves beyond their garrets and, "from the bottom," they realized themselves as such, as a counterculture. In this unofficial stream there were some internal currents, enthusiasts of fight, resistance, and impulsive actions that rose above the struggle. There were also traders, true pioneers of market relations. I will note in the name of memory that ironically all of them participated in the erosion of the system. The system was equally tested by the expressed subjective social protest and by modern gesture, which in the West is already chrestomathic. They were perceived by the Soviet state at that time as non-conformant, and as attempts to organize an art market at the expense of the government.

The enthusiasts of fight, understanding the hopelessness of resistance to the government, confident enough in their power to smuggle out Solzhenitsyn from the country; could not overcome temptations to compete with him. On September 15th, 1974, on the vacant land in Belyayev, a group of Moscow artists under the management of O. Rabina and A. Gleyzera attempted to expose their works outdoors. Communication problems with the spectators were hardly the most important hurdle. The political action was planned as a test of power. Everyone was interested in the reaction of the government. Will it permit it? Or will it forbid it? Or, simply, will it just not pay attention? Overall, of course, everyone was expecting a ban. The activists of the underground movement were for long ready to "divorce" the government; up to emigrating. Western journalists were witnesses to the "undoing of families". The result exceeded all expectations. The provoked state answered wildly, inadequately, and barbarously by sending bulldozers that destroyed pictures; the short-lived caddishness of drunken combatants, and of course arrests. And although subsequently the authorities, shocked by international indignation, tried to recuperate from the events, and even tolerated subsequent unofficial exhibitions, the matter was over.

For many artists, the following fifteen years, up to the dismantling of the Soviet system, were years of a forced stay. Certainly, for many it was possible to choose residence - the flow of artist-emigrants throughout the period never stopped. Others were forced to settle into areas where communication with the object of their bygone love was not possible.

Thus, the most inveterate enemies of the government were long gone. The most commercially oriented attempted to extract benefit from their dissent, and thus were able to nurse their internal independence. This was perhaps the best way out of the situation. Shwartzman, Shteynberg, Krasnopevtsev, Yankilevskiy searched for their identity in the field of metaphysics. Other representatives of the first generation of unofficial artists as Kabakov worked with "available reality" in its entirely Soviet-specific character. They espoused an escapist program: escape from reality into metaphysics. This strategy ironically assumes a definite dependence on the same reality. Bulatov objectified in his pictures the structures of ordinary consciousness; Pivovarov's bars insisted on the impersonality of his experience, i.e. the inferior narration of numerous and faceless "tellers" that recognize the presence of Soviet reality. Moreover, in every way possible the accentuated the objectivity of its existence both in and out of consciousness. This removed problem of fighting with this reality, denying it, displacing it from the consciousness.

Liberal tradition compared the Soviet state with the Leviathan. Accordingly, it was necessary to fight to bring about its destruction, and that is what the artists of modern type and gesture did. The strategy of post-modern artists and it is precisely to this way of thinking that someone like Kabakov belonged, was different. His freedom was not in the struggle against the Leviathan-state, but in the selection of a position with respect to himself.

This position can exist conceptually, analytically, playful, distant, and near, up to mimicry - Kabakov's authorization of the production of the combines of the Artistic Fund, breadwinners of entire generations of Soviet artists; the restless customers of senseless objects. It can be distinguished by the type of positioning inside or it is outside of the "Soviet body". The artist, simply stated, can accept the role of researcher, who observes the Leviathan through a powerful gaze from the side, and can perceive himself in the skin, and in the belly of the beast. But mainly, this can be only personal, private, the author's own, selected by the artist, but not by the state, and not depending on the imposed rules of the game. This strategy of post-modern artists of not getting involved was seen as the highest degree of internal freedom.

The following generation of the representatives of the school of Moscow Conceptualism did not resist the temptation to pull the decrepit beast by its

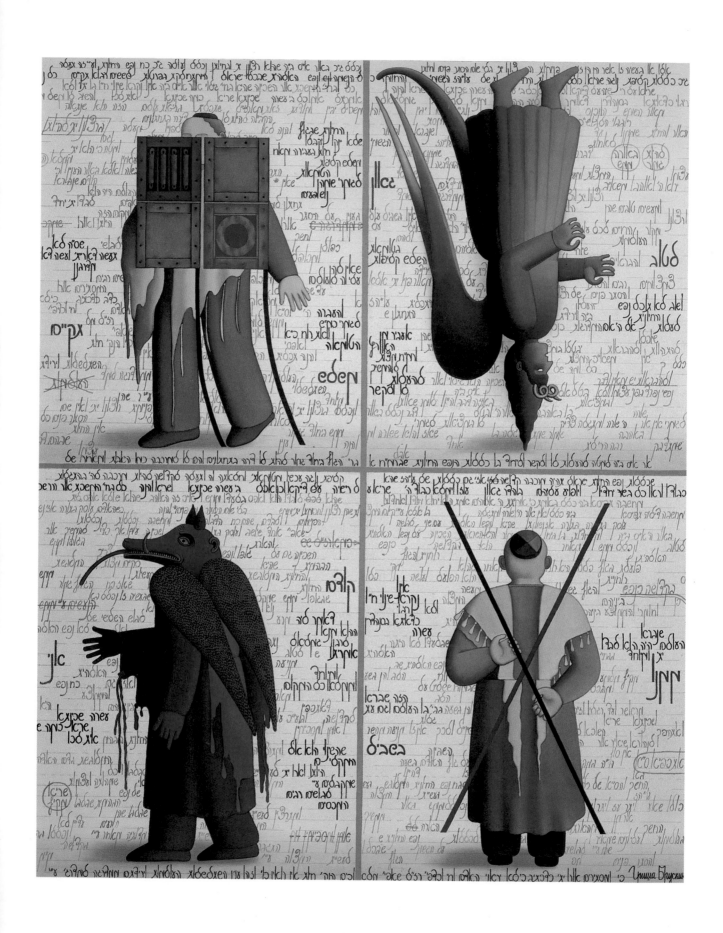

Grisha Bruskin
Message 3, 1989-90
(oil on linen, 56" X 44")

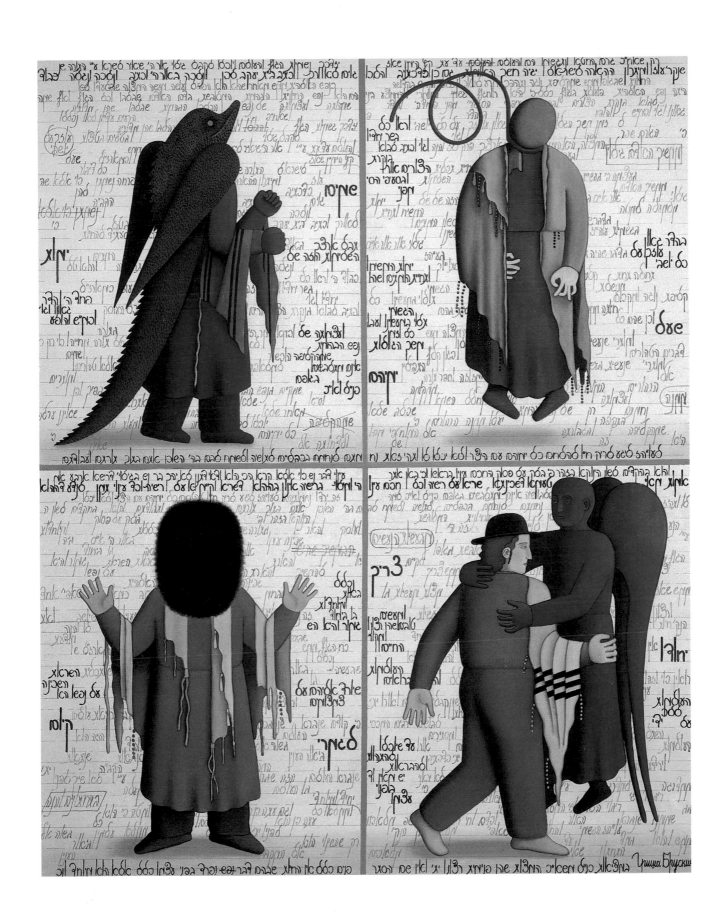

Grisha Bruskin
Message 5, 1989-90
(oil on linen, 56" X 44")

Leonid Sokov
Old and New Russian-Soviet Symbols, 1989-90
(mixed media on paper, 30 1/2" X 22 1/2")

Ilya Kabakov
Mikhailov: Others, 1973
(colored pencil and ink on paper, 12" X 8")
Yuri and Nelly Traisman Collection

tail. The "social artists" - Komar & Melamid, Kosolapov, Sokov, Bruskin - manipulated Soviet myths and ideas: deconstructed them, splitting, reversing them. There was no sacred cow on which "social artists" would not comment: Lenin and Stalin, cruiser "Aurora" and mausoleum, State Coats of Arms and rewards, pioneer ("scout") necktie and board of honor. The "social artists" were the last artists of Soviet origin: with all their conceptual nihilism they were truly touched by Soviet unconscious. Even on the strange, New York soil (practically all of them emigrated in the 1980s) this habit of living in viscous Soviet experience did not cease, and for nearly ten years it fed their art.

Alexander Kosolapov,
Malevich Sold Here, c. 1996
(lithograph, 24" X 30")

Much has been written on underground or so-called "other art". For me, in the context of this specific exhibition the most intriguing aspect is aesthetic. From a contemporary perspective, not a historical-cultural one, all the exponents, beyond the historical merit in the establishment and victory of independent art, and beyond the regalia and their accompanying myths, proved that nothing was certain about the holy cows.

They were active, developing artists with strictly individual directions, grappling with very important contemporary cultural problems. And if one finds certain similarities between them, which hint at the process of selection of these particular artists, I suggest that one looks at aspects of the modern artistic strategies, especially that they, as previously noted, in many ways establish the character of today's "representational wave". All the presented masters are individuals by principle (in fact, in this individual self-identification, the right for personal feelings in the stream of art is one of the victories of the *Shestidesyatniki*. At the same time, in the most common coordinates of artistic strategy, this art continues to sustain the urgently greedy, and from the ironic post-modern position somewhat naēve, belief of the *Shestidesyatniki* in an artistic spirit that possesses not only form-creating but also life-building potential.

Leonid Sokov
Stalin and Marilyn, 1990
(bronze and mixed media
on paper mounted on
board, 30 1/2" X 22 1/2")

This impulse, through the very many changes, continues to feed the conviction of artists in the transcendental character of their work. Thus, the major issue, which concerned Yankilevskiy for decades, is more powerful: the opposition between universal spatial energy and the sum of local, group and personal energies. His anthropomorphic figures throb, like under a current, trying to bring in the element of order or harmony into unstructured elements. In the same way, Bulatov with all his concentration on textual practice, on a visualization of an ideology, maintains this transcendental impulse, with which his calculated, weighed, strictly organized compositions that glimmer in the twilight, not yielding to logical interpretation with metaphysical meanings. Rabin, the key figure of the Moscow underground, subsequently organically connected to the Paris School, preserved in its dense, expressive painting a quality of alogism that could be defined, following Pasternak as Moscow devilry. In the last few years M. Odnoralov has become an active artist. In his art, the spirit of new figuration is accentuated by the solid, and thus revives the currents of that articulated spirituality, with which this generation first joined the art stage.

New connections are forming because of the proximity of the works of these artists with the works of masters not mentioned above. Nesterova always developed individually, in spite the various attempts to appropriate her creations. It is more interesting to observe her connection with the installations of other generations and directions, especially with the Conceptual, thoughtful project, which outwardly contradicts her particularly picturesque and emotional artwork.

In the context of this exhibition it becomes clear, why she constantly demands respect among the producers of urgent art. In principle the indecipherable character inherent in the persistent repetition of motives, in the increasing alogism of the depicted situations is seen if not as an esoteric practice, but by the reflection of metaphysical conditions. In a sense, it is the mark of a potentially conceptual project.

Translated by Janina Dubizhanskaya

RUSSIAN REMEMBRANCE: A SOLARIAN PROJECT • JEFF LIPSCHUTZ

Tsarist Russia romanticized itself with the transparent fantasy of enduring love, a current flowing in a closed, continuous loop between "the peasants" and their exalted, absolutist rulers. It was a performance the Romanovs played to the hilt over three centuries, highlighted finally by a photogenic waltz, replete with cockade and delirium, off the arc of history and into unmarked graves.

Long deprived of basic rights and hope, most Romanov subjects thus greeted the 1917 Revolution as a miracle on earth. But the utopian ardor of the artists of the new Soviet Union - Yesinin, Tatlin, Stepanova, Mayakovsky, El Lissitzsky, Popova - having been borne onto the Soviet and world stages so wondrously, was soon cooled by Stalin's indelicate attentions, then summarily destroyed. Administered by the Party and its security labyrinth, "Uncle Joe's" cultural shock treatment was only slowed down by Hitler's expansionist horrors. The mother land's memory lay flattened under the boot heels of competing tyrants. Stalin lived on, as did the purges, and even after Khrushchev, the Soviet people endured twenty more years of gray-faced henchmen, with their dog masks, tin ears, and still-thriving Gulagian anti-history. Another door burst open with the fall of the Berlin Wall. The people blinked and saw their empire, equal parts myth and reality, reflected in the Wall's absence; they blinked again, and, impossibly, the empire was gone.

In this traveling exhibition, curated by Alexandre Gertsman, contemporary Russian artists - born in Russia and the former Soviet republics, and living in Russia, the U.S., and Europe - continue to find the touchstone for their work in their land of origin. As a lost, unburied mother, and a violent, half-remembered father, the past lives on for these artists, at once all-loving and all-damning, unfathomably deep-eyed, thin-skinned, thick-bearded, jeweled, sickly, fearsomely life-giving, deathless. More than the unformed present, it is this unfinished past, with its myriad, imagined meanings, that captivates them, and brims their ranks with metaphysicians, anti-ideologists, ideologists, gnostics, Russianists, kabbalists, tragedians, arch-humorists and fabulists.

Andrei Tarkovsky's 1971 film, *Solaris*, based on the novel by Polish writer, Stanislaw Lem, posits a planet where tragically failed human experiences are re-lived, where the darkest memories of visitors to the planet are materialized as living, human copies. Experiences never resolved are recycled to seduce, confuse, and ultimately unhinge an assortment of researchers.

This construction of reality as temporarily fluid and layered is not, however, specifically circular, as in Proust, nor is it gift-wrapped with a Proustian ribbon of final redemption. Rather, in addition to personal happiness, human "progress" is on the table in the high stakes drama of Lem/Tarkovsky. Tarkovsky visually immerses us in the windowless womb of the space station's library, panning past busts of Socrates and the Venus de Milo, paintings by Brueghel, and a death mask of Beethoven - a clear, stage by stage, cultural eschatology.

Solaris is a land of unfinished business, where lost loves, dreams and ambitions grip visitors in a bear hug as massive and stupefying as the aura of Brando's glutenous Kurtz, looming and shadowed in his upriver kingdom of last resort in *Apocalypse Now*.

Alexandre Gertsman has observed that the twentieth century was marked by "one of mankind's grandest utopian dreams - a dream of a great commune and a great nation." For Americans, Gertsman's reference to Russia will surely be held up to the mirror of our own national experience. Teddy Roosevelt and Woodrow Wilson were hardly visionaries on the scale of Lenin, but when it came to laying the groundwork for America's modern, or modernist, destiny, they did shepherd us out of our post-Civil War wanderings and steer us unflinchingly toward the headwaters of "The American Century."

This exhibition is comprised of contemporary Russian art. Its nostalgia is for the entire Russian past, but especially for the early twentieth century avant-garde, whose, in the words of Hilton Kramer, "...vanguard art was cruelly destroyed by the revolutionary regime on which all its hopes had once been lavished." This is the known yet astonishing difference between Russian and American modernism. Russian avant-garde art was essentially political; it grew as a child of and sustainer to the new regime. Russia didn't merely dabble in revolutionary visions of the future, as did most early twentieth century American and European modernists; its avant-garde utterly believed in and diligently worked for their dreamed futures, putting away pan-Russian hegemonism, Kirgiz, Tajik, or Jewish ethnocentric programs and destinies, volunteering, to build a classless, gender-equal, ethnicity-less utopia.

Americans in the first decades of the twentieth century certainly were possessed of a growing and formidable national self-concept. One need only look at New York and Chicago to see what was happening, on the ground, vis a vis the scale of the American modernist vision. Nonetheless, our modernism developed, not as a political program, but as an artistic response to its previous art, to a pervasive frustration at its externally perceived cultural provincialism, and to interfaces with European modernist painting and sculpture, as in the 1913 Armory Show.

By the mid-1940s and through the 1950s, more than twenty years after Russian modernism had been crushed, the New York School had come to represent the pinnacle and "triumph" of American modernism. Gone was the cosmical whimsy of early Arthur Dove, the primary, rhythmic joy of Marsden Hartley's New Mexico landscapes, O'Keefe's magical, pristine, New York nightscapes. The new American painting was larger, more committed to a universal, truly non-objective abstraction, and to a thoroughly tragic philosophical tone.

That said, when has the American artist, even in the foulest backwash of the McCarthy era, been compelled - in the words of Solaris' Snouth - "...to strive for a god he fears and doesn't want," or risk being destroyed by the very ideals he expresses in his art?

Historically, Americans and American artists have been more populist, practical, and less metaphysical, than their Russian counterparts. Especially since its demise, it is clear how metaphysical the supposedly political program of "godless Marxism" always was. And it is clear that Russian artists are currently so invested in the past, and especially, in the Russian modernist past's conceptions of the future, because so much was promised, and almost materialized.

Russian contemporary artists are both wary and committed. As a Solaris pilot, Burton, says, "Have I the right to give up striving for Contact, for which we humans have been striving for so long?" This impetus toward a Large Answer is still distinctively Russian from an American perspective. Don't we strive to solve problems, more than construct mega-theories? As a white-coated, Scientific Authority figure in Solaris declares, "By not moving Forward, we move Backward." Would a representative American even bother to voice such a seeming redundancy? We live to thrive in a popular, mass culture present, with respect to which the past must be healed (repaired) in the same way that the present and future must (and can) be fixed.

The assumption of the mantle of tragic expression in its art lasted for approximately two decades in America. Pop came on in the sixties with its hypnotic barber poles of self-love and mockery, was embraced and has never let go. Shuffled off to Buffalo's Albright-Knox Gallery, and to art history's spaces and databases everywhere, went Rothko's clouds and Still's upthrusting (Solarian?) whorls, replaced by freeways, soup cans, bikinis, pies, hairdos. With American multiculturalism and post-modernism, Pop remains the visual reference and language of choice.

The concerns of Russian contemporary artists are distinct from those of their American counterparts, as examplified by Semyon Faibisovich and Vitaly Dlugy. Russians may see us as obsessed with the present, and opportunistically antagonistic toward a politicized past. In the 1970's, Komar and Melamid appropriated American Pop Art as a conceptual principle, and contextualized its consumerist, "now" iconography as a window onto a multi-layered, tragic, and nostalgic history.

In his later work, Philip Guston was comparably successful, in refracting Pop language backwards, via cartoons of the thirties, to a lost, nostalgic era: pre-New York School and pre-War. Guston directed our gaze away from the art world - away from Warhol, and from Greenberg, more importantly. He pointed to the experiences of his Odessa-born father, and himself, as immigrant and second-generation Americans, respectively. The father was seen as a haunted ragman (and suicide-to-be) in the new country; Philip, the son, as a studio-bound working stiff, buoyed by his labors and troubled affections.

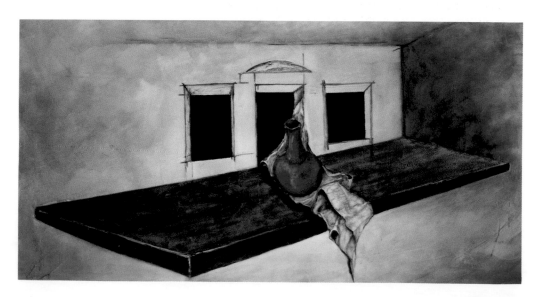

Vitaly Dlugy
Alone, from "Last Supper" series, 1990
(oil on canvas, 42" X 80")

Semyon Faibisovich
We Care..., 1990
(oil on canvas, 76" X 62")

Among the many artists in the "Remembrance" exhibit, Natalya Nesterova most closely parallels the idiosyncratic poignancy of Guston's. But while Guston, the New York Old-Leftist, imbues his characters with a pink, proletarian tenderness, Nesterova's Moscow-based figures are more bleached and less cuddly. Their semi-naëve treatment lends them pathos, but they are primarily strange, enlivened, yet simultaneously paralyzed by social realities, and by the Russian fixation on the idea of society.

If it is difficult to imagine American art without its themes of self-love and -mockery, Russian art remains unthinkable absent its own twin obsessions: lost time and tragic fate. In "Remembrance: Russian Post-Modern Nostalgia," we are most of all invited to question. We may ask which came first: America's democratic, utilitarian paradise of the twentieth and twenty-first centuries, or the Russians' metaphysical rupture of pre-modern society from everything which has followed?

Rimma Gerlovina and Valeriy Gerlovin

Born in Moscow, and live in New York.

Selected Exhibitions

1999   Sawhill Gallery, James Madison University, Harrisonburg

1997   McDonough Museum of Art, Youngstown

   Pensacola Museum of Art, Pensacola

1995   Steinbaum Krauss Gallery, New York

   Robert Brown Gallery, Washington, DC

   University Art Museum, Lafayette

1994   New Orleans Museum of Art, New Orleans

   Olive DeLuce Gallery, Northwest Missouri University, Maryville

1993   Jacksonville Museum of Art, Jacksonville

   University of Colorado Gallery, Boulder

   Selsby Gallery, Ringling School of Art, Sarasota

1989   MIT List Visual Arts Center, Cambridge

   Anderson Gallery, Virginia Commonwealth University, Richmond

Selected Public Collections

J. Paul Getty Museum, Malibu

International Center of Photography, New York

Polaroid Corporation, Cambridge

The Jewish Museum, New York

Museum of the Berlin Wall, Berlin

Museum of Modern Art (MoMA), New York

The School of the Art Institute of Chicago, Chicago

Addison Gallery of American Art, Andover

Jane Voorhees Zimmerli Art Museum, New Brunswick

Tsaritsyno Museum, Moscow

Ministry of Culture "Moscow Collection" (Leonid Talochkin collection)

Paris Audiovisuel, Paris

Massachusetts Institute of Technology, Cambridge

Queensland Art Gallery, Brisbane

Denver Art Museum, Denver

Progressive Corporation, Cleveland

Prudential Corporation, Newark

Australian National Gallery, Canberra

Tate Gallery, London

Rimma Gerlovina & Valeriy Gerlovin
REAL, 1989
(color coupler print, 19" X 19")

Rimma Gerlovina & Valeriy Gerlovin
Tree of Life, 1989
(Ektacolor print in stainless steel frame, 87 1/2" X 48")

Rimma Gerlovina & Valeriy Gerlovin
Eve, 1993-95
(Ektacolor print in aluminum frame with pencil drawing, 79 1/2" X 39")

Ilya Kabakov

Born in Dniepropetrovsk, and lives in New York.

Selected Exhibitions

2002 "Espacio Concepto," Fundacion Joan Miro, Barcelona

2001 "Ilya Kabakov," Galerie Clara Maria Sels GmbH, Dusseldorf

1999 "Ilya Kabakov – Der Rote Waggon," Museum Weisbaden, Weisbaden

"Fragilite-Absurdite," Galerie Clara Maria Sels GmbH, Dusseldorf

"Die Zerbrechlichkeit des Seins," Galerie Clara Maria Sels GmbH, Dusseldorf

"Retrospective," Kunstmuseum, Bern

1998 "Crossings/Traversées," National Gallery of Canada, Ottawa

"The Palace of Projects" (with Emilia Kabakov), The Roundhouse, London; Upper Campfield Market, Manchester; The Crystal Palace, Museo Nacional Centro de Arte Reina Sofia, Madrid

"The Children's Hospital" (with Emilia Kabakov), Irish Museum of Modern Art, Dublin

1997 "We Were In Kyoto" (installation with Emlia Kabakov) for "Future, Present, Past," XLVII Venice Biennale, Venice

1996 "Sur le toit/Op het dak (On the Roof)," Palais des Beaux-Arts, Brussels

"Healing with Paintings," Kunsthalle, Hamburg

1995 "C'est ici que nous vivons (We Are Living Here)," Centre Georges Pompidou, Paris

"The Rope of Life and Other Installations," Museum fur Moderne Kunst, Frankfurt
"No Water" (permanent installation), Austrian Museum of Applied Arts (MAK), Vienna

1994 "Tyrannei des Schonen: Architektur der Stalin-Zeit," Austrian Museum of Applied Arts (MAK), Vienna

1993 "Von Malewitsch bis Kabakov," Kunsthalle, Köln

"Het Grote Archief (The Big Archive)," Stedelijk Museum, Amsterdam

"The Red Pavilion," installation for XLV Venice Biennale

1992 "Documenta IX," Kassel (Germany)

"Life with an Idiot," The Netherlands Opera-Hetmuziek Theater, Amsterdam (costumes and sets by Ilya Kabakov)

"Unhung Painting" (permanent installation), Ludwig Museum, Koln

"Das Leben der Fleigen (The Life of Flies)," Kunstverein, Köln

1991 "Dislocations," Museum of Modern Art (MoMA), New York

Selected Public Collections

Kunstmuseum, Berlin

The State Tretyakov Gallery, Moscow

The State Pushkin Museum of Fine Arts, Moscow

Duke University Art Museum, Durham

The Jewish Museum, New York

Museum of Modern Art (MoMA), New York

Ilya Kabakov
The Test of Destiny, 1997
(mixed media, 22 1/4" X 20 3/8" X 20 1/2")
Yuri and Nelly Traisman Collection

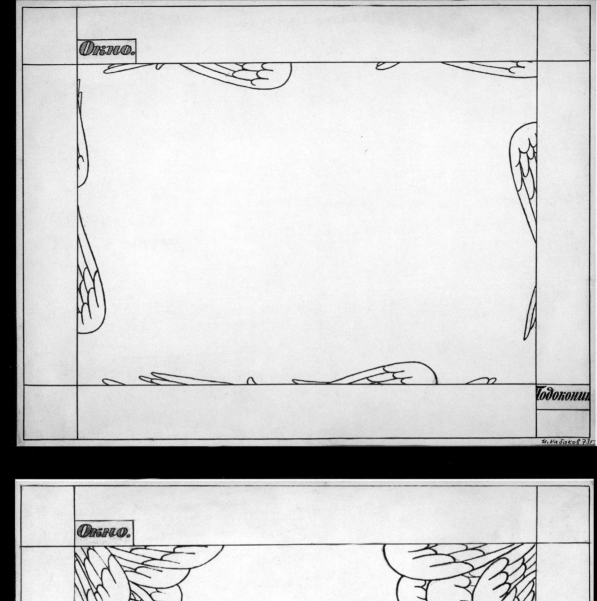

ERIC BULATOV

Born in Sverdlovsk, and lives in Paris.

Selected Exhibitions

1998 "Forbidden Art: The Russian Postwar Avant-Garde," (trav., cat.) College of Design, Pasadena, CA; The State Russian Museum, St. Petersburg (1999); The State Tretyakov Gallery, Moscow; Miami University Art Museum, Oxford, OH

1996 "Russian Jewish Artists: In a Century of Change, 1890-1990," The Jewish Museum, New York (cat.)

1990 Stedelijk Museum, Amsterdam

1989 Kunsthalle Zurich – Parkett Verlag and Centre Georges Pompidou, Paris (trav. Germany)

Institute of Contemporary Art, London (trav. U.S.)

1988 "Aperto 88," Venice Biennale

1987 "Direct from Moscow," Phyllis Kind Gallery, New York

"The Artist and His Time," Exhibition space, Kachirskoёe Road, Moscow

"Sots Art," The New Museum of Contemporary Art, New York (trav.)

1984 "Sots Art," Semaphore Gallery, New York

Selected Public Collections

Musee National d'Art Moderne - Centre Georges Pompidou, Paris

Musee Maillol - Foundation Dina Vierny, Paris

Anne Voorhees Zimmerli Art Museum, New Brunswick

Selected Publications

Urs Stahel, "Eric Bulatov. Vielleicht Bloss eine Atempause," *Art: Das Kunstmagazin*, Hamburg, No. 1, January 1988, pp. 102-103

Christoph Schenker, "Eric Bulatov," *Noema*, No. 17, 1988, pp. 64-71

Jürg ALtweg, "Räume des Lichts Erik Bulatov," *Frankfurter Allgemeine Magazin*, Frankfurt, 11 March 1988, pp. 12-20

Eric Bulatov, "Malevich et l'espace," *A-YA*, No. 5, Elancourt, 1983, pp.26-31

"Erik Bulatov," Teknitcheskaёa Esteika, No. 6, Moscow, 1982, p.17

Vassili Patsioukov, "Erik Bulatov, Edouard Steinberg," *A-YA*, No. 3, Elancourt, 1981, pp. 14
Boris Groys, Interview with Erik Bulatov, *A-YA*, (Review of non-official Russian art), No. 1, Elancourt, 1979, pp.26-33

Dominique Bozo, J. Nicholson, "Boulatov," *Chronique de l'art vivant*, No. 23, Paris, September 1971, p.13

Eric Bulatov
House, 1992
(oil on canvas, 71" X 71")
Yuri and Nelly Traisman Collection

VITALY KOMAR AND ALEXANDER MELAMID

Born in Moscow, and live in New York.

Selected Exhibitions

2000   "Russian Art of 1980-2000," Pace University Arts Center, New York (cat.)

1999   Russia's Presentation, Venice Biennial, Venice

"Museums as Muse," Museum of Modern Art (MoMA), New York

1998   Schon-Haosslich, Kunsthalle, Vienna

"Modernism and Post-Modernism: Russian Art of the Ending Millennium," (trav. U.S. – 2001)

1997   Venice Biennial, Venice - Arsenale

People's Choice, Ludwig Museum of Modern Art, Koln

1996   People's Choice, Alternative Museum, New York

1995   "Russian Jewish Artists in a Century of Change, 1890-1990," The Jewish Museum, New York

"Temporarily Possessed," The New Museum, New York

1994   Alternative Museum, New York

1991   "Black Lights," Stedelijk Museum, Amsterdam

1990   "Komar and Melamid," Brooklyn Museum, New York

1989   "Image World: Art and Media Culture," Whitney Museum of American Art, New York

1988   "Commited to Print," Museum of Modern Art (MoMA), New York

"Hommage-Demontage," Neue Galerie - Ludwig Forum, Aachen

Museum Moderner Kunst, Vienna

Selected Public Collections

Metropolitan Museum of Art, New York

Museum of Modern Art (MoMA), New York

Solomon R. Guggenheim Museum, New York

Hirshhorn Museum and Sculpture Garden, Washington, D.C.

Whitney Museum of American Art, New York

Victoria and Albert Museum, London

The Australian National Gallery, Canberra

The Canadian National Gallery, Ottawa

The Jewish Museum, New York

Museum of Modern Art, Vienna

Wadsworth Atheneum, Hartford

Israel Museum, Jerusalem

Museum Ludwig of Modern Art, Koln

The State Tretyakov Gallery Museum, Moscow

The State Russian Museum, St. Petersburg

Komar & Melamid
The Toast (Triptych), from "Anarchistic Synthesism" series, 1985
(mixed media, 3 panels, 72" X 106" overall)

Komar & Melamid
Blindman's Bluff, from "Nostalgic Socialist Realism" series, 1982-83
(tempera and oil on canvas, 72" X 47")
The Metropolitan Museum of Art, New York

Komar & Melamid
I Saw Stalin Once When I Was a Child, from "Nostalgic Socialist Realism" series, 1982-82
(oil on canvas, 72" X 54")
The Museum of Modern Art, New York

BORIS MIKHAILOV

Born in Kharkov, and lives in Kharkov and Berlin.

Selected Exhibitions

2000 "Berlin," Fotomuseum Winterthur, Switzerland (cat.)

12th Biennale of Sydney, Australia (cat.)

Museum of Contemporary Art, Ljubljana, Slovenia (cat.)

"Bons Baisers de Russie Caronne" Festival, Toulouse

"Positions, Attitudes, Actions: Social and Political Commitment in Photography,"for the Foto BiĎnnale of Sydney, Sydney

"How You Look at It," Photographs of the 20th Century, SPrengel Museum, Hannover (trav. Cat.)

BMW Collection, Hamburg & Munich (cat.)

"Boris Mikhailov: 2000 Hasselblad Award Winner," Hasselblad Center, Göteborg

"Boris Mikhailov," The Photographers' Gallery, London

1999 "Future is Now: Ukranian Art in the Nineties," Museum of Contemporary Art, Zagreb

"After the Wall: Art and Culture in post-Communist Europe," Moderna Museet, Stockholm (cat. trav.)

"By the Ground," Museum of Modern Art, Ljunljana

"Boris Mikhailov," Museo Querini Stampalia, Venice (cat.)

"Global Conceptualism: Points of Origin, 1950s-1980s," Queens Museum of Art, New York (trav. cat.)

1998 Nobuyoshi Araki & Boris Mikhailov," Satani Gallery, Tokyo

1996 "Russian Jewish Artists in a Century of Change: 1890-1990," The Jewish Museum, New York (cat.)

1993 "New Photography 9," The Museum of Modern Art (MoMA), New York

Selected Public Collections

Metropolitan Museum of Art, New York

Museum of Modern Art (MoMA), New York

Stedelijk Museum, Amsterdam

Kunstbibliothek, Berlin

San Francisco Museum of Modern Art, San Francisco

Jane Voorhees Zimmerli Art Museum, New Brunswick

Zürich University, Zürich

Kiasma – Museum of Contemporary Art, Helsinki

DAAD Berliner Künstlerprogramm, Berlin

Centro d'Arte Contemporanea, Castello di Rivara

Maison Européene de la Photographie, Paris

Portuguese Center for Photography

Museum of Contemporary Art, Zagreb

Boris Mikhailov
Red Series, 1960s-70s (color photograph, 12" X 8")
Norton and Nancy Dodge Collection of Russian Non-Conformist Art
Jane Voorhees Zimmerli Art Museum
Rutgers, The State University of New Jersey, New Brunswick

Boris Mikhailov
From "Salt Lake" series, 1986
(Ektacolor print)
Pace/MacGill Gallery, New York

Boris Mikhailov
Untitled, n.d. (color photograph, 12" X 17 1/2")
Norton and Nancy Dodge Collection of Russian Non-Conformist Art
Jane Voorhees Zimmerli Art Museum
Rutgers, The State University of New Jersey, New Brunswick

LEV POLIAKOV

Born in St. Petersburg (Leningrad), and lives in New York.

Selected Exhibitions

2000 Herbert Hoover Pavilion, Stanford University, Stanford (CA)

1992 Stadtmuseum, Munich

1987 Fotogalerie, Schwanenburg – Köln

1983 "Faces of Russia," Nikon House, New York

Selected Public Collections

Metropolitan Museum of Art, New York

New York Public Library

Publications

1992 Hanser, Carl. *Die Russen* (Munich)

1991 Giroux, Farrar Straus. *Russia – A Portrait* (New York)

1980 Fotogalerie. *Die Verlorenen Inseln* (Schwanenburg – Köln)

Kaiser, Robert. EP Dutton. *Russia From the Inside* (New York)

Additional publishing and covers: *Time Magazine, Basen Blatt, The New York Times, Nurnberger Zeitung, Paris Match, Die Welt, L'Espresso, Heilbronner Stimme, Vogue, Letter International. The New York Times Magazine, Photo Technik International, Suddeutsche Zeitung, Foto Vedio, Osttauringer Zeitung;* Knopf, Random House, Doubleday, and Macmillan.

Lev Poliakov
Parade, 1965
(gelatin silver print, 20" X 24")

Lev Poliakov
Leader, 1965
(gelatin silver print, 11" X 14")

Lev Poliakov
Akimov's Funeral, 1968
(gelatin silver print, 11" X 14")

ALEXANDER KOSOLAPOV

Born in Moscow, and lives in New York.

Selected Exhibitions

1996   "Tribute to Gorbachev," University of Connecticut, Storrs

"Here and There, Then and Now: Contemporary Artists from the Former Soviet Union," National Jewish Museum, Washington, D.C.

1995   "Temporarily Possessed," New Museum, New York

"Russian Jewish Artists in a Century of Change, 1890-1990," The Jewish Museum, New York

1994   Gallerie Vorsetzen, Hamburg

Cetinjski Biennial, Montenegro

"El Magico Mundo De Mickey Mouse," Cuartel Conde Duque, Madrid; Palau Sant Jordi, Barcelona

"Before 'Neo' and After 'Post'," Lehman College Art Gallery, City University of New York, New York

1993   Galerie Inge Baecker, Köln

1992   "Ex USSR," Groninger Museum, Holland

"Sots Art," Lenin Museum, Moscow

1991   "From Thaw to Perestroika," Setagaya Art Museum, Tokyo

"Kunst Europa 1991 - USSR," Kunstverein, Hanover

"Art and Publicity," Du Sezon Museum, Tokyo and Centre Georges Pompidou, Paris (1990)

1990   "The Objects," Stedelijk Museum, Amsterdam and Tsaritsino Museum of Contemporary Art, Moscow

"Another Art 1956-76," TheState Tretiakov Gallery, Moscow

1989   "Transit: Russian Art Between the East and West," The State Russian Museum, St. Petersburg, Russia and Fine Arts Museum of Long Island, Hempstead

"D&D," Kunstverein, Hamburg

"Reagan: American Icon," Central Gallery, Bucknell University, Lewisburg and Reading Public Museum and Art Gallery, Reading (PN)

Galerie Inge Baecker, Köln

Selected Public Collections

Museum of Modern Art (MoMA), New York

The State Russian Museum, St. Petersburg

The State Pushkin Museum of Fine Arts, Moscow

National Jewish Museum, Washington, D.C.

Albertina Museum, Vienna

New York Public Library - Prints Collection, New York

Jane Voorhees Zimmerli Art Museum, New Brunswick

Hofstra Museum, Hempstead

Alexander Kosolapov
Molotov Cocktail, 1990
(silk screen, 25 1/2" X 30 1/2")

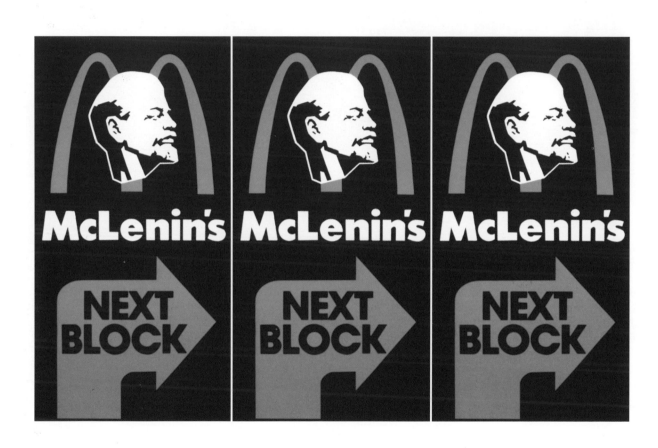

Alexander Kosolapov
McLenin's (Triptych), 1991
(silk screen on vinyl, 45 1/2"X 70 1/2" overall)

Alexander Kosolapov
Workers' Club USSR (Triptych), 1985
(oil mixed media on canvas, 114" X 68" overall)

LEONID SOKOV

Born in Mikhalevo, and lives in New York.

Selected Exhibitions

2001   Venice Biennale

1999   Palais des Nations, Geneva

"Forbidden Art," The State Russian Museum, St. Petersburg (trav. cat.)

The State Tretyakov Gallery, Moscow

1998   "2 x Immortal: Elvis + Marilyn" (trav. cat.)

Institute of Contemporary Art, Boston

Pennsylvania Academy of the Fine Arts, Philadelphia

Mint Museum of Art, Charlotte

Columbus Museum of Art, Columbus

Baltimore Museum of Art, Baltimore

Honolulu Academy of Art, Honolulu

Hokkaido-Obihiro Museum of Art, Hokkaido (cat.)

Daimaru Museum, Umeda, Osaka

Takamatsu City Museum of Art, Takamatsu, Shikoku

SoHo Museum of Art, New York

Mitsukoshi Museum of Art, Fukuoka

Kumamoto Prefectural Museum of Art, Kyushu

1997   Galleria Severiarte, Bologna

1996   D'Arte Contemporanea, Cesena-Cevenatico (cat.)

1995   Farsettiarte, Prato (cat.)

"Kunstlewerkstatt," Kraftemessen, Munich

"Kunst in verborgenen Documenten," Halle Kassel, Kassel (cat.)

"Kwangju Biennale," South Korea (cat.)

Selected Public Collections

Metropolitan Museum of Art, New York

Musee National d'Art Moderne - Centre Georges Pompidou, Paris

Solomon R. Guggenheim Museum, New York

National Gallery of Australia, Sydney

The Pushkin Museum of Fine Art, Moscow

The State Tretyakov Gallery, Moscow

The State Russian Museum, St. Petersburg

Jane Vorhees Zimmerli Art Museum, New Brunswic

Duke University Museum of Art, Durham

Leonid Sokov
Meeting of Two Sculptures, 1990
(bronze, 19" X 5 1/2" X 15")
Solomon R. Guggenheim Museum, New York

GRISHA BRUSKIN

Born in Moscow, and lives in New York.

Selected Exhibitions

2001   "Grisha Bruskin: Life is Everywhere," The State Russian Musem, St. Petersburg and The
State Pushkin Museum of Fine Arts, Moscow

2000   "Grisha Bruskin," Marlborough Gallery, Boca Raton

1999   "Grisha Bruskin: Leben uber Alles," Gallery Andy Jullien, Zurich

"Grisha Bruskin: Life is Everywhere," Marlborough Gallery, New York

1997   "Grisha Bruskin: Revisions," Marlborough Gallery, New York

1996   "Grisha Bruskin: Mythical Imagery," Meyerovich Gallery, San Francisco

"On Paper," Marlborough Gallery, New York

1995   "Grisha Bruskin," Museo Nacional de Bellas Artes, Buenos Aires

"Russian Jewish Artists in a Century of Change 1890-1990," The Jewish Museum, New York

1994   "Grisha Bruskin: Metamorphoses," Meyerovich Gallery, San Francisco

"Grisha Bruskin: General Instruction and Other Works," Marlborough Gallery, New York

1993   "Grisha Bruskin: Paintings, Drawings, and Sculptures," Struve Gallery, Chicago

"Grisha Bruskin: Painting, Sculpture, Prints," Linda Farris Gallery, Seattle

"Grisha Bruskin: General Instruction/Lev Rubinstein: Another Name," The State Pushkin
Museum of Fine Arts, Moscow and The State Russian Museum, St. Petersburg

"Drawing the Line Against AIDS," Venice Biennale, Venice

Solomon R. Guggenheim Museum-SoHo, New York

"Von Malewitsch bis Kabakov: Russiche Avantgarde im 20, Jahrhundert, Eine Ausstellung
des Museums Ludwig," Joseph-Haubrich-Kunsthalle, Köln

"Post-Modernism and Tradition," The State Tretyakov Gallery, Moscow

"A la decouverte...de collections romandes," Musée d'art Contemporain, Pully/Lausanne

1992   "Grisha Bruskin," Alex Lachmann Gallery, Köln

1991   "Grisha Bruskin: A Personal Mythology," Erika Meyerovich Gallery, San Francisco

"Grisha Bruskin: Paintings and Sculpture," Hokin Gallery, Palm Beach

Selected Public Collections

Museum of Modern Art (MoMA), New York

The Jewish Museum, New York

Art Institute of Chicago, Chicago

The State Tretyakov Gallery, Moscow

Museum Ludwig of Modern Art, Köln

Nationale Galeria de Arte, Caracas

The State Pushkin Museum of Fine Arts, Moscow

The State Russian Museum, St. Petersburg

Israel Museum, Jerusalem

[left]
Grisha Bruskin
Broken Love, 2002
(plaster, height 48")

[right]
Grisha Bruskin
Hasid, 2002
(plaster, height 48")

Grisha Bruskin
Alefbet-Lexica I, 1995
(oil on canvas, 46 3/8" X 35 1/8")
Mr. and Mrs. Mark Wilf Collection

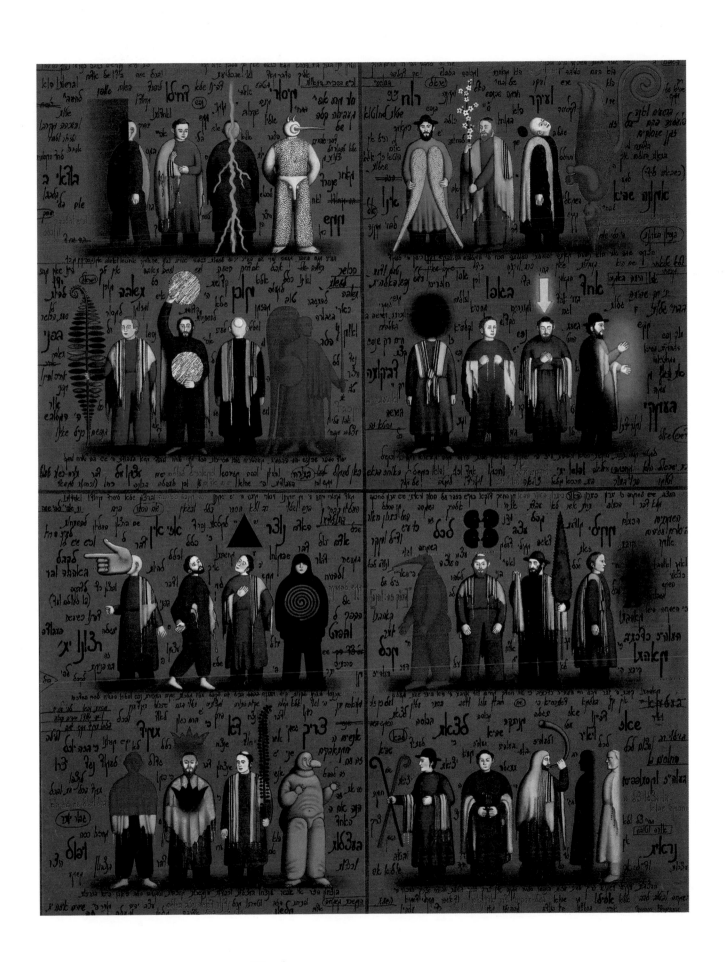

Grisha Bruskin
Alefbet-Lexica II, 1995
(oil on canvas, 46 3/8" X 35 1/8")
Mr. and Mrs. Mark Wilf Collection

SVETLANA KOPYSTIANSKY

Born in Voronezh, and lives in Berlin.

Selected Exhibitions

1997   "The Fiction," Ludwig Forum for International Art, Aachen (trav., cat)

1995   Biennale di Venezia, "Club Berlin," Teatro Malibran, Venice

"ORIENT/ ATION, The Vision of Art in a Paradoxical World," The 4th International Istanbul Biennale, Istanbul (cat.)

"Materials for Art," Kunsthalle, Düsseldorf

"Non-Comformists, Russia 1957-1993," Wilhelm-Hack Museum, Ludwigshafen; Doccumenta-Halle; State Lindenau-Museum, Alternberg

"Women Artists in the Collection," Art Gallery of New South Wales, Sydney (cat.)

"Allegorie de la Richesse," St. Lois de la Sapetriere, Paris

"Landscape," Mittelrhein-Museum, Koblenz, traveling to Museum Schloss Murgk an der Saale (1996) and Haus au Waldsee, Berlin (cat.)

"Memento," Haus am Wannsse, Berlin; and Stadtgalerie im Sophienhot, Kiel (cat.)

1994   "The Library," Kunsthalle, Düsseldorf (cat.)

"Peripatheticos," Kunsthalle, Helsinki

"Die Bibliothek," Berlinische Galerie im Martin-Gropius-Bau, Berlin Oulu Art Museum, Oulu (Finland)

"Cocido y Crudo," Museu National Centro de Arte Reina Sofia, Madrid (cat.)

"JETZTZEIT," Kunsthalle, Vienna; and De Appel, Amsterdam (cat.)

22nd International Biennale of Sao Paulo, Sao Paulo (cat.)

"Di Carta e d'Altro, Libri d'artista," Centro per l'Arte Contemporanea Luigi Pecci, Prato

"Memento," State Gallery, Prague (cat.)

"Biennale Balticum 94," Rauma museum, Rauma Finland (cat.)

"Great Gifts, Great Patrons," Art Gallery of New South Wales, Sydney (cat.)

"Allegorie de la RIchesse," Bibliotheca di Storia Moderna e Contemporanea, Rome

"Untitled Untitles," Granary Books Gallery, New York

1993   "The Discovery..." FAE Museum of Contemporary Art, Pully, Lausanne (cat.)

"Future Perfect," Heiligerkreuzerhof, Hochschule fur Angewandte Kunst, Vienna (cat.)

"Monumental Propaganda," World Financial Center, New York and traveled (cat.)

"Ludwig's Lust," Germanisches Nationalmuseum, Nurnberg (cat.)

"Adresse Provisoire," Musee de la poste, Paris (cat.)

"After Perestroika: Kitchenmaids or Stateswoman," Centre international d'Art Contemporain, Montreal (trav. U.S., Canada, and Germany)

Selected Public Collections

Metropolitan Museum of Art, New York

Museum Ludwig of Modern Art, Koln

Jane Voorhees Zimmerli Art Museum, New Brunswick

Svetlana Kopystiansky
Landscape I, 1984 (oil on canvas, 31 2/5" X 39 1/3")
Norton and Nancy Dodge Collection of Russian Non-Conformist Art
Jane Voorhees Zimmerli Art Museum
Rutgers, The State University of New Jersey, New Brunswick

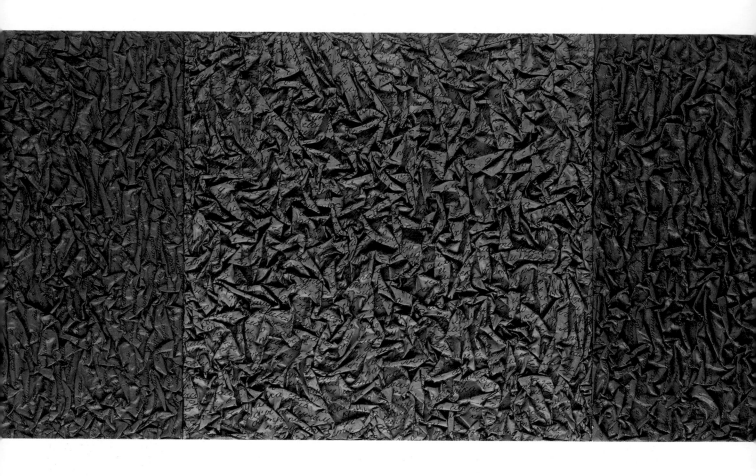

Svetlana Kopystiansky
Story, 1989
(oil on canvas, 40" X 80")
Yuri and Nelly Traisman Collection

Svetlana Kopystiansky
Landscape II, 1984 (oil on canvas, 31 2/5" X 39 1/3")
Norton and Nancy Dodge Collection of Russian Non-Conformist Art
Jane Voorhees Zimmerli Art Museum
Rutgers, The State University Museum of New Jersey

MIKHAIL ROGINSKY

Born in Moscow, and lives in Paris.

Selected Exhibitions

1992 Discoveries 92, Galerie J. Alyskewycz., Grand Palais, Paris
1991 "Drougoye Iskoustvo," (Another Art), Moscow
"From degel to Perestroika," Tokyo & Galerie Farideh Cadot, Paris
Galerie Jorge Alyskewycz, Paris
1990 "Transit," (trav.) New York, Leningrad, Moscow
"Object" (trav.) Moscow, Amsterdam
"Art Decoded," Galerie S. de Beyrie and Bourse du Commerce, Paris
"Heads," Galerie Jorge Alyskewycz, Paris
1989 "Humor and Revolution," Cannes and Gerona
1988 FIAC 88, Galerie Lavrov, Paris
"Five Russians in Toulouse," Aerospace Culture Center, Toulouse
Galerie Georges Lavrov, Paris
1987 Studio Gallery, Hamburg
1986 Art Fair 86, Galerie Geroges Lavrov, BČle (Switzerland)
Galerie Geroges Lavrov, Paris
1985 FIAC 85, Galerie Georges Lavrov, Paris
1984 "Countries and Countrysides," DRAC Campagne-Ardennes, Reims
1983 Galerie Geroges Lavrov
1982 Salon de Montrouge
Bineth Gallerie, Tel-Aviv
1981 "Works on Paper," Villeparisis
1980 Cité Internationale des Arts, Paris
1978 "Russians in Paris," Galerie Bellint, Paris
1977 Twelve Artists in the Moscow Painter's Union
1976 Ministry of Culture, Moscow
1975 "Apartment Exhibition," Moscow
Non-comformist Painters – "Apartment Exhibition," Moscow
1967 "Thirty Years of Soviet Theatre," Moscow
1964 "Unofficial Exhibition of Four Non-conformist Painters," Moscow
1962 "Moscow Decorative Theatre Painters," Moscow

Selected Public Collections

The State Tretyakov Gallery, Moscow
Musee Maillol - Foundation Dina Vierny, Paris
Jane Voorhees Zimmerli Art Museum, New Brunswick
National Jewish Museum, Washington, D.C.

Mikhail Roginsky
Catastrophe, 1986
(oil on canvas, 60" X 80")

Mikhail Roginsky
Fire, 1985
(oil on canvas, 40" X 50")

Mikhail Roginsky
Untitled, 1985
(oil and mixed media on canvas, 80" X 60")

OLEG VASSILIEV

Born in Moscow, and lives in New York.

Selected Exhibitions

1999   "Oleg Vassiliev: On Black Paper, 1994-1997," Wake Forest University FineArts Gallery, Winston-Salem, NC (trav. - 2001, U.S.)

"Forbidden Art: The Postwar Russian Avant-garde," The State Russian Museum, St. Petersburg; The Tretyakov Gallery, Moscow

"It's the Real Thing: Soviet and Post-Soviet Sots Art and American Pop Art," Frederick R. Weisman Museum of Art, University of Minnesota, Minneapolis

1997   "Oleg Vassiliev," Phoenix Gallery, Moscow

1995   "Oleg Vassiliev: Windows of Memory," Sloane Gallery, Denver

"From Gulag to Glasnost: Noncomformist Art from the Soviet Union,"

"The Damaged Utopia," Kraftemessen, Munich

"A Mosca...A Mosca," Museum Kunstverein, Karlsruhe

1994   "No! and the Conformists: Faces of the Soviet Art of the 50s to 80s," Dunikowski Museum, Plac Krolikarni (Poland); The State Russian Museum, St. Petersburg

"Stalin's Choice: Soviet Socialist Realism 1932-1956," PS1 Museum, New York

"Zeitgenossen," Kunstmusem, Bern

1993   "Oleg Vassiliev: Recent Works," Phyllis Kind Gallery, New York

"Tre Kunstneres syn pa Tjekov," Norsk-Russisk Center, Kirkenes

FAE Musée d'Art Contemporain - Pully, Lausanne

"Temporary Address from Contemporary Russian Art," Post Museum, Paris

1992   "A Mosca...A Mosca," Villa Campolietto, Herculaneum (Italy); Museum of Modern Art, Bologna

"Three Points of View," Center for Contemporary Art, Moscow

"Eric Bulatov/Oleg Vassiliev," Phyllis Kind Gallery, New York

Selected Public Collections

Kunstmuseum, Bern

The State Tretyakov Gallery, Moscow

Museum Ludwig of Modern Art, Koln

Drezden Staatliche Kunst Gallery, Drezden

The Pushkin Museum of Fine Arts, Moscow

The State Russian Museum, St. Petersburg

Denver Art Museum, Denver

Duke University Museum of Art, Durham

Art Museum of the University of Kentucky, Lexington

Jane Voorhees Zimmerli Art Museum, New Brunswick

Norsko-Russik Kunst Center, Kirkenes

Oleg Vassiliev
From "Home With an Attic" series, 1991
(lithograph 29 3/4" X 21 1/2")

Oleg Vassiliev
From "Home With an Attic" series, 1991
(lithograph 29 3/4" X 21 1/2" each)

Oleg Vassiliev
From "Home With an Attic" series, 1991
(lithograph 29 3/4" X 21 1/2" each)

VLADIMIR YANKILEVSKY

Born in Moscow, and lives in Paris.

Selected Exhibitions

1995   "Russian Jewish Artists in a Century of Change, 1890-1990," The Jewish Museum, New York

   "Boulatov, Kabakov, Yankilevsky, Musee Maillol - Foundation Dina Vierny, Paris e
   "From Gulag to Glasnost: Nonconformist Art from the Soviet Union," Jane Voorhees
   Zimmerli Art Museum, New Brunswick

   Gift from the Collection Ludwig to the Russian Museum (Inauguration), The State Russian
   Museum, St. Petersburg

1994   Ludwig Forum for Contemporary Art, Aachen

   FIAC, Leonard Hutton Galleries, Paris

1993   "Russische Avantgarde im 20 Jahrhundert," Ludwig Collection, Museum Ludwig of Modern
   Art, Koln

   "Art of Postmodernism," The State Tretyakov Gallery, Moscow

   "Works on Paper," Museum Bochum, Bochum, Germany and Gallery Bargera, Hamburg

1991   "Eastern Art - Western Art," Ludwig Forum for Contemporary Art, Aachen

1990   "The Other Art: 1956-1976," The State Tretyakov Gallery, Moscow and The State Russian
   Museum, St. Petersburg

   "The Quest for Self-Expression: Paintings in Moscow and Leningrad 1965-1990," (trav. U.S.)

1988   "Russian Avant-Garde and Soviet Contemporary Art," Sotheby's, Moscow

   Art Olympiad, National Museum of Contemporary Art, Seoul

   "Ich Lebe - Ich Sehe, Kunstler der achtziger Jahre," Moscow

1987   Photography and Book, Central House of Artists, Moscow

   Object I, Malaya Gruzinskaya Exhibition Hall, Moscow

1986   "Scientific and Technological Revolution and Art," Central House of Artists, Moscow

1985   "Century Graphic Art from Hungarian Collections," Museum of Fine Arts, Budapest

Selected Public Collections

Musee National d'Art Moderne, Centre Georges Pompidou, Paris

Ludwig Forum for Contemporary Art, Aachen

Prague National Gallery, Prague

The State Pushkin Museum of Fine Arts, Moscow

The State Russian Museum, St. Petersburg

The State Treryakov Gallery, Moscow

Staatliche Kunstsammlungen Dresden, Dresden

Budapest Fine Arts Museum, Budapest

Museum Bochum, Bochum (Germany)

Frederick R. Weisman Art Foundation, Los Angeles

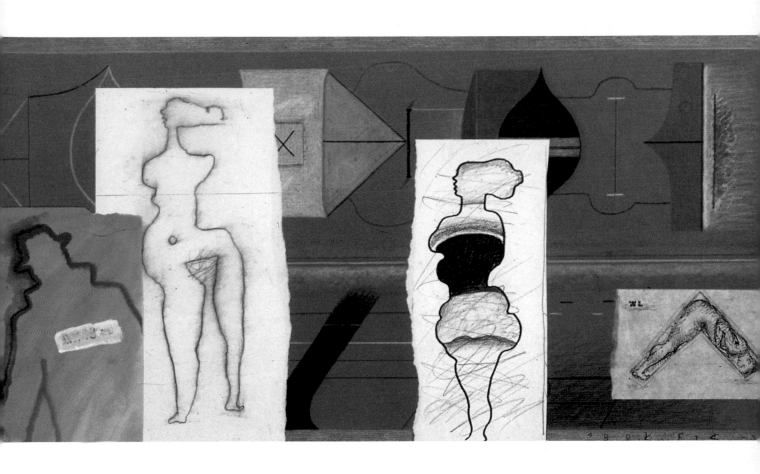

Vladimir Yankilevsky
#10, from "City" series, 1992
(collage/mixed media on cardboard, 25" X 76")

SLAVA TSUKERMAN

Born in Moscow, and lives in New York.

Selected Filmography

1970s *Vaudville About Vaudville* (tv musical comedy, tv)

A Night for Reflection (with Innokentiy Smoktunovsky)

Once Upon a Time there Lived Russians in Jerusalem (first prize – telecine film festival, Hollywood)

1983 *Liquid Sky* (international cult classic; still exhibited yearly at film festivals worldwide)

2000 *Impoverished of Lees*

2002 *Pomagranate, Garnet Bracelet, Band* (Gatchine Russian film festival; Kinotavr Festival first prize; American Anthology of Film Archives, New York)

Slava Tsukerman, 1999
Komar & Melamid and Van Gogh
(still captures, from video)

SEMYON FAIBISOVICH

Born and lives in Moscow.

Selected Exhibitions

2002   Moscow Photo Biennial

"Actual Moscow Painting," New Manezh, Moscow

2001   "Everything has Its Time," Andrei Zakharov Museum, Moscow

"Semyon Faibisovich: My Windows," Moscow Museum of Photography

"Exhibition of New Acquisitions," Moscow House of Photography

2000   "XX Century Art," The State Tretyakov Gallery

1999   Museum of Contemporary Art, Central House of Artists

"Act 99," Museum of Art, Weslts (Austria) and Manezh, Moscow

"Post-War Russian Avant-garde, The State Russian Museum, St. Petersburg," The State Tretyakov Gallery, Moscow and Miami University Museum

1995   "Nonconformist Art from the Soviet Union," Jane Voorhees Zimmerli Art Museum, New Brunswick

1994   Before "'Neo' and After Post: Contemporary Russian Initiative," Lehman College Art Gallery, New York

1993   "M'Aidez/Mayday," Phyllis Kind Gallery, New York

1990   "Semyon Faibisovich," Phyllis Kind Gallery, New York

Chicago International Art Fair, Chicago

"Adaptation and Negation of Socialist Realism," The Aldrich Museum of Art

1989   "Von Der Revolution zur Perestroika," Russian Art from the Ludwig Museums, Musee d'Art Moderne, Saint Atin (Switzerland)

1988   "Ich Be - Ich sche, Art museumsk there is another arragement

International Art Fair, Chicago

Art Fair, Koln

"Glasnost," Kunsthalle, Emden

1976   Exhibitions in the basement of the Moscow Union of Graphic Artists (through 1988)

Selected Public Collections

The State Tretyakov Gallery, Moscow

The State Russian Museums, St. Petersburg

Jane Voorhees Zimmerli Art Museum, New Brunswick

Semyon Faibisovich
May Day, 1990
(oil on canvas, 90" X 76 1/2")

Semyon Faibisovich
#1, from "Line for Vodka" series, 1990
(oil on canvas, 76" X 90")

Semyon Faibisovich
#2, from "Line for Vodka" series, 1990
(oil on canvas, 76" X 90")

MICHAEL ODNORALOV

Born in Moscow, and lives in New York.

Selected Exhibitions

2000   "Russian Art of 1980-200," Pace University Arts Center, New York (cat.)

1999   "Russian Art in America: Kabakov, Komar & Melamid, Nesterova, Odnoralov," IntArt Museum of Upstate New York, Oneonta, New York

1998   "Modernism and Post-modernism: Russian Art of the Ending Millennium," The Yager Museum, Hartwick College, Oneonta (trav. cat.)

1997   "Michael Odnoralov: Alice From the Lower East Side," Lehman College Art Gallery, CUNY, New York

1996   "Here and There, Then and Now: Contemporary Artists from the Former Soviet Union," National Jewish Museum, Washington, D.C.

1994   "Artists to Russia," Literaturnaya Gazette Exhibition, Moscow

1991   "Paintings Return to Russia," Central House of Artists, Moscow

1990   "Different Art," The State Tretyakov Gallery, Moscow

1988   "Russian Contemporary Still-life," C.A.S.E. Museum of Contemporary Russian Art, New Jersey

1984   "Michael Odnoralov," TAT Gallery, New York

1983   Unofficial Art from the Former Soviet Union, Cannon Rotunda and Russell Rotunda of the Congress Building, Capitol Hill, Washington, D.C.

1976   Exhibition of Moscow Avant-garde Artists, Union of Artists if the Soviet Union, Moscow

1975   "Avant-garde Art Exhibition," Pavilion at the National Economic Achievements Exposition, Moscow

1974   "Open Air Exhibition of Unofficial Art - Bulldozer Exhibition," Moscow

1973   Exhibition of Young Soviet Artists, USA (trav.)

1969   Cafe "Blue Bird", Moscow

1967   Exhibition of Young Soviet Artists, Germany

1966   Michael Odnoralov, Union of Artists of the Soviet Union, Moscow

1964   Michael Odnoralov and Eduard Shteinberg, Moscow University, Moscow

1961   Exhibition of Moscow Artists, Tarusa

1960   Avant-garde Art Exhibition, Moscow

SELECTED PUBLIC COLLECTIONS

The State Tretyakov Gallery, Moscow

National Jewish Museum, Washington, D.C.

The Duke Museum of Art, Duke University, Durham

Jane Voorhees Zimmerli Art Museum, New Brunswick

Hofstra Museum, Hempstead

Michael Odnoralov
German Doll, 2003
(oil on canvas, 40" X 40")

NATALYA NESTEROVA

Born and lives in Moscow.

Selected Exhibitions

2000   "Natalya Nesterova: Russian Wanderings," National Jewish Museum, Washington D.C. (trav. U.S. - 2001)

1999   "Natalya Nesterova: Last Supper," National Tretyakov Gallery, Moscow and Tallinn Museum of Fine Arts, Estonia

1998   "Modernism and Post-modernism: Russian Art of the Ending Millennium," (trav. U.S. 2001)

1996   "Here and There, Then and Now: Contemporary Artists from the Former Soviet Union," National Jewish Museum, Washington, D.C.

1995   "From Gulag to Glasnost: Nonconformist Art from the Soviet Union," Jane Voorhees Zimmerli Art Museum, New Brunswick

1994   "Before 'Neo' and After 'Post'," Lehman College Art Gallery, City University of New York, New York

1993   "Four Russian Messages: Carnival and Drama," Evergreen House Museum, The Johns Hopkins University Art Museum, Baltimore

1992   "Natalya Nesterova," The Montreal Museum of Fine Arts, Montreal

"Natalya Nesterova," The State Tretyakov Gallery Museum, Moscow

1991   "Artistas Rusos Contemporanes," Santiago De Compostela, Auditorio De Galicia (Spain)

1990   "Contemporary Soviet Art," The Aldrich Museum of Contemporary Art, Ridgefield, CT

"The Quest for Self-Expression: Paintings in Moscow and Leningrad 1965-1990," Columbus Museum of Art, Columbus (travl. U.S. – 1991)

1989   "Natalya Nesterova and Lazar Gadaev," Central Exhibition Hall Manez, Moscow

1988   "Russian Avant-Garde and Soviet Contemporary Art," Sotheby's, Moscow

"Art Contemporain Sovietique," A.R.C.O., Madrid

Chicago International Art Fair, Chicago

1987   "Art Contemporain Sovietique," F.I.A.C., Galerie de France, Paris

"Six Moscow Artists," Riga, Latvia and Tallinn, Estonia

Selected Public Collections

Solomon R. Guggenheim Museum, New York

Ludwig Forum for Contemporary Art, Aachen

The Jewish Museum, New York

The Montreal Museum of Fine Art, Montreal

Museum of Contemporary Art, Seoul

The State Russian Museum, St. Petersburg

The State Tretyakov Gallery Museum, Moscow

Slovak National Gallery, Bratislava

Museum of Contemporary Art - Ludwig Museum, Budapest

Natalya Nesterova
Three People on a Ladder, 2002
(oil on canvas, 68" X 39 1/3")

Natalya Nesterova
Youth, Maturity, Old Age, 2003
(oil on canvas, 68" X 40")

Natalya Nesterova
Carelessness, Hope, Despair, 2003
(oil on canvas, 68" X 40")

Natalya Nesterova
Dancing People, 1990
(oil on canvas, 64" X 64")

Natalya Nesterova
People on the Shore, 1990
(oil on canvas, 64" X 64")

OSCAR RABIN

Born in Moscow, and lives in Paris.

Selected Exhibitions

1996   "Face a L'histoire: L'artiste moderne devant l'evenement historique 1933-1996," Musee National d'Art Moderne - Centre Georges Pompidou, Paris

"Here and There, Then and Now: Contemporary Artists from the Former Soviet Union," National Jewish Museum, Washington, D.C.

1995   Inaugural Exhibition, Maillol Museum - Foundation Dina Vierny, Paris

"Russian Jewish Artists in a Century of Change, 1890-1990," The Jewish Museum, New York

"From Gulag to Glasnost: Nonconformist Art from the Soviet Union," Jane Voorhees Zimmerli Art Museum, New Brunswick

1993   "Oscar Rabin: A Retrospective," The State Russian Museum, St. Petersburg

1989   "Transit: Russian Art Between the East and West," The State Russian Museum, St. Petersburg, Russia; and Fine Arts Museum of Long Island, Hempstead, N.Y.

1975   Exhibition in the House of Artists, Moscow

1974   "Buldozer Exhibition," Izmailovo Park, Moscow

1970   "Nuove correnti a Mosca," Museo Belle Arti, Lugano

1969   "Neue Moskauer Schule," Galerie Pananti, Florence

1967   "Quindici Giovani Pittori Moscoviti," Galeria II Segno, Rome

1966   16 Moscow Artists, Sopot, Posnan, and Stettin, Poland

1964   "Aspekte der zeitgenossischen sowjeischen Kunst," Grosvenor Gallery, London

Selected Public Collections

The State Russian Museum, St. Petersburg

The State Tretiakov Gallery Museum, Moscow

Musee Maillol - Foundation Dina Vierny, Paris

Jane Voorheese Zimmerli Art Museum, New Brunswick

Oscar Rabin
Ashtray, 1992
(mixed media on canvas, 52" X 76")

VITALY DLUGY

Born in Moscow, and lived in New York until 1990.

Selected Exhibitions

2000 "Russian Art of 1980-2000," Pace University Arts Center, New York

1998 "Modernism and Post-Modernism: Russian Art of the Ending Millennium" (trav. U.S. – 2001)

1996 "Here and There, Then and Now: Contemporary Artists from the Former Soviet Union," National Jewish Museum, Washington, D.C.

1994 "Before 'Neo' and after 'Post'," Lehman College Art Gallery, City University of New York, New York

"Still-life," The State Tretyakov Gallery, Moscow

"Meaning as a Second Language," Chase Freedman Gallery, West Hartford and Norman and Sarah Brown Art Gallery, Baltimore

"Russian Art is the Mainstream," Gallery One, West Hartford

1990 "The Russian Experiment," Castle Gallery, College of New Rochelle, Rochelle

1988 "Contemporary Russian Art," Musee de l'art Russe Contemporain, Paris

1984 "Moscow-Paris-New York," Gallery Marie-Therese Cochin, Paris

1983 "Unofficial Art from the Former Soviet Union," Cannon Rotunda and Russell Rotunda of the Congress Building, Capitol Hill, Washington, D.C.

1981 "25 Years of Soviet Unofficial Art," Museum of Soviet Unofficial Art, Jersey City and Museum of Contemporary Russian Art, Montgeron

1980 "Unofficial Russian Art: First Biennale of Russian Painters," Centre des Arts et Loisirs du Vesine, Vesine and Salone Fieristico, Rimini

"Nicht-offisielle Kunst," Kunsthause, Salzburg; Kunst Center, Vienna; and Kunst Center, Bregens

1979 "Moscow-Paris," Musee d'art Russe Contemporain," Montgeron

1978 "Modern Unofficial Soviet Art," Municipal Museum, Tokyo

"Unofficial Russian Art," Musee de Vieux Chateaux, Laval; Musee des Beaux, Tours; Musee des Beaux-Arts de Chartres, Chartres

Selected Public Collections

The National Jewish Museum, Washington, D.C.

State Russian Museum, St. Petersburg

Duke Museum of Art, The Duke University, Durham

Jane Voorhees Zimmerli Art Museum, New Brunswick

Hofstra Museum, Hempstead

Vitaly Dlugy
Chair – Quote, 1986
(oil on canvas, 32" X 26")

Naum Kazhdan

Born in St. Petersburg (Leningrad), and lives in New York.

Career Highlights

1981   *New York Times* studio photographer (to present)

1977   Freelance photographer for *New York Post*, *Star*, *Stash Record*, *Metro Studio*, and *F-Stop*

1972   Sovexpert film exporter

       Lenconcert Gosconcert official photographer

       Our Fashion fashion photographer, Leningrad

1967   photographic design of the museum of revolution in Leningrad

Mr. Kazhdan is a Soviet expert and participated in the photographic design of the "Water" section in the Soviet Pavilion at the 1967 International Exhibition in Montreal. In addition to noted publishings, word with journals of maritime engineering and various advertising magazines. He has also photographed for a number of jazz magazines, including *Jazz* (Poland), and *Downbeat* (U.S.), and has won distinction at the International Jazz Photography Festival in Warsaw.

His photographs exist in a number of renowned private and corporate collections worldwide.

Naum Kazhdan
Russian Museum Opening (Triptych), 1995
(triple silver gelatin print, 16" X 20")

Naum Kazhdan
Walking Chimneys (Triptych), 2002
(triple silver gelatin print, 16" X 20")

Naum Kazhdan
Crime at the Met (Triptych), 1995
(triple silver gelatin print, 16" X 20")

GENIA CHEF

Born in Aktyubinsk, and lives in Berlin.

Selected Exhibitions

2003　"Foreign Visions," Starke Foundation, Berlin and Museum of Contemporary Art, Skopje (cat.)

"Berlin," German Ministery of Foreign Affairs, Berlin (cat.)

"Naked before Gods," Parnu Museum of New Art, Parnu (Estonia)

2002　"Shock and Show" Festival of International Contemporary Art, Trieste (cat.)

"A Brief History of Collage and Assemblage," Jane Voorhees Zimmerli Art Museum, New Brunswick (cat.)

"Artists of the Ideal", Palazzo Forti, Verona (cat.)

Freud`s Dreams Museum, St. Petersburg

2001　"Between Earth and Heaven," Museum of Modern Art, Ostende (Belgium, cat.)

Galerie Eikelmann, Dusseldorf

2000　"Jesus Christus," The State Russian Museum, St. Petersburg and The Vatican Museum, San Marino (cat.)

"The Myths of King Ludwig II of Bavaria," Novaja Akademija, St. Petersburg

1999　"Play and Passion", The State Russian Museum, St. Petersburg (cat.)

King-Ludwig II Musical Theatre, Fussen

Galeria Maria Salvat, Barcelona

1998　"American Pop Art - Russian Sots Art", Frederick Weisman Art Museum, Minnesota University, Minneapolis (cat.)

"Neo-Academism and Elektronic Art," Novaja Akademija, St. Petersburg (cat.)

Selected Public Collections

The State Russian Museum, St. Petersburg

Jane Voorhees Zimmerli Art Museum, New Brunswick

Museum of Contemporary Art, Skopje

Museum Haus am Checkpoint Charlie, Berlin

Freud`s Dreams Museum, St. Petersburg

Italian Culture Institute, Berlin

Museum of European Art, Buffalo

Hofstra Museum, Hempstead

Church of Cadaques, Spain

St.Georg-Church, Ulm

Ministery of Post and Communication, Ulm

Genia Chef
Millennium II (Triptych), 2003
(digital print, light box in three dimensions, 15 3/4" X 31 1/2" X 2 1/3")

Genia Chef
The Eternal City, 2003
(digital print, light box in three dimensions, 15 3/4" X 31 1/2" X 2 1/3")

Genia Chef
Foro Imperiale, 2001
(digital print, light box in three dimensions, 15 3/4" X 31 1/2" X 2 1/3")

VLADIMIR CLAVIJO-TELEPNEV

Born and lives in Moscow.

Selected Exhibitions

2003   Art Play Gallery, Moscow

Lumier Gallery, Moscow

"Fashion and Style," Photo Biennale, Manege Gallery, Moscow

Photo Show, Petrovsky Passage Gallery, Moscow

Photo Show, Museum of Modern History, Moscow

2002   New Manege, Moscow

Smolensky Passage Gallery, Moscow

International Photo Biennale, Manege Gallery, Moscow

"Propagandistic and Romantic: Contemporary Russian Photography," Allen Priebe Gallery, University of Wisconsin-Oshkosh

"Photography of Interior," Lumier Gallery, Moscow

2001   Central Gallery, Tbilisi (Georgia)

The Glinka Museum of Musical Culture, Moscow

International Photo Biennale, Manege Gallery, Moscow

Annual Photo Exhibition, Photography Center, Moscow

"Photo," Museum of History, Moscow

"Photography,: Central Photo House, Moscow

"Fashion and Style," Second International Photo Festival, New Manege, Moscow

2000   "Young Artists," Kuznetczky Bridge Gallery, Moscow

International Photo Biennale – 2000, Central Artist's House, Moscow

"Y2K-aotic: Uncensored All-media Salon Show," OIA Salon Show, New York

1999   "Belgrade," Republic Beefeater Gallery, Moscow

"Architecture and Design," Central Artist's House, Moscow

Pushkin, Central Artist's House, Moscow

1998   International Photo Biennale – 1998, Manege Gallery, Moscow

1997   "Moscow Artists," Kunetczky Most 20 Gallery, Moscow

1996   "Moscow Artists," Manege Gallery, Moscow

1995   "Moscow Artists," Kunetczky Most 11 Gallery, Moscow

1994   Salon Show, Photography Center, Moscow

1993   Association of Moscow Artists, Grekov Studio, Moscow

Salon Show, Gallery Levkas, Moscow; Riga; Kaliningrad; Petrozavodsk

Moscow Artists, Parliament Center, Moscow

1992   Group Show, Krasnaya Presnaya Exhibition Center, Moscow

1991   "The Game for Four Hands," Salon Show-Chernishevski Street, Moscow

Group Show, Manege Gallery, Moscow

1986   Fall Salon Show, Kunetczky Most 20 Gallery, Moscow

Vladimir Clavijo-Telepnev
Death of Marat, 2003
(photograph, 38" X 41 1/2")

Vladimir Clavijo-Telepnev
#1, from "Suffering" series, 1999-2002
(photograph, approx. 66"X 48")

Vladimir Clavijo-Telepnev
#2, from "Suffering" series, 1999-2002
(photograph, approx. 66"X 48")

Vladimir Clavijo-Telepnev
#3, from "Suffering" series, 1999-2002
(photograph, approx. 66"X 48")

Vladimir Clavijo-Telepnev
#4, from "Suffering" series, 1999-2002
(photograph, approx. 66"X 48")